D1141288

PRINCIPLES OF CHRISTIAN WORSHIP

PRINCIPLES OF CHRISTIAN WORSHIP

With Special Reference to the Free Churches

By

RAYMOND ABBA

M.A. (*Cantab. and Sydney*), B.D. (*Melbourne*)

LONDON

OXFORD UNIVERSITY PRESS

NEW YORK TORONTO MELBOURNE

1957

Oxford University Press, Amen House, London E.C.4
GLASGOW NEW YORK TORONTO MELBOURNE WELLINGTON
BOMBAY CALCUTTA MADRAS KARACHI
CAPE TOWN IBADAN NAIROBI ACCRA SINGAPORE

PRINTED IN GREAT BRITAIN

To my
FATHER AND MOTHER
with gratitude and
affection

PREFACE

THIS book reproduces the substance of a course of lectures delivered during the Lent and Trinity Terms 1954 at St. Andrew's College in the University of Sydney. The lectures were attended by Congregational, Methodist and Presbyterian theological students, at whose request they have been prepared for publication. While the general scheme of the course has been retained, the original material of the lectures has been supplemented and the whole rewritten and expanded.

The book is intended, not as a comprehensive survey, but rather as an introduction to the subject and a practical guide for the minister in the conduct of worship. The approach is theological and historical but I have attempted throughout to relate both theology and history to present-day practice. Too often the ordering of worship is determined by questions of expediency instead of by reference to first principles. There is, as I have tried to show, a theology of worship which has practical implications in such matters as the structure of a service, the place of Scripture lessons, psalms and hymns, the ordering of public prayer, and the administration of the sacraments. Guidance for further reading will be found in the footnotes and bibliography.

An outline such as this may also be of value in stimulating liturgical discussion, particularly within the Free Churches, with whose worship it is primarily concerned. The coming together in the Ecumenical Movement of Churches with widely differing liturgical traditions has made the need for such discussion urgent. As the Report of the Faith and Order Commission on Ways of Worship points out, 'In worship we meet the problem, nay rather the sin of the disunion of the Church in its sharpest form' (p. 23), and 'At long last we are beginning to see that, measured by the standards of the New Testament and the early Church, none of our current ways of worship is fully adequate' (p. 21). Although this volume is written from the point of view of a Free Churchman, it is hoped that it may be of interest and value to members of other communions also and contribute to a fuller understanding between Christians of different liturgical traditions.

I welcome the opportunity of acknowledging my deep indebtedness to my father, the Reverend Herbert W. Abba, under whose long and distinguished ministry of forty-five years at Latimer Congregational Church, Beverley, I first experienced the reality of worship in spirit and in truth. These chapters owe much to his wise teaching and rich experience. I am also indebted to my friend, the Reverend C. Maitland Elliss, of Narromine, New South Wales, who has freely shared with me, on many occasions, his encyclopaedic knowledge of liturgical principles and practice.

My thanks are especially due to my former colleague, Archdeacon D. E. W. Harrison, of Sheffield, for the care with which he read and criticized my manuscript and for very helpful suggestions and advice; also to the Reverend Professor W. D. Maxwell, who most kindly read the book in typescript on the eve of his departure to Grahamstown, South Africa, and made many valuable comments. I am grateful to the staff of the Oxford University Press for a meticulous accuracy and unfailing helpfulness in its publication; to the Reverend E. T. Donald James, of Wolverhampton, for the generous use of his library; and to my wife for much valuable assistance and constructive criticism, not forgetting her ready help in the reading and correction of the proofs.

RAYMOND ABBA

WOLVERHAMPTON,
April, 1957.

ACKNOWLEDGEMENTS

GRATEFUL acknowledgement is made to the following publishers and others for permission to use extracts from copyright publications:

Geoffrey Bles Ltd., for an extract from *Letters to Young Churches* by J. B. Phillips; the Cambridge University Press for extracts from *Christian Doctrine* by J. S. Whale; the Clarendon Press, Oxford, for extracts from essays by R. S. Franks, J. S. Whale, W. H. Cadman, C. H. Dodd, K. L. Parry and the Editor, from *Christian Worship* edited by Nathaniel Micklem; the Edinburgh House Press for an extract from *What is a Living Church?* by J. S. Whale; the Epworth Press, London, for extracts from *The Hymns of Wesley and Watts* by Bernard L. Manning, and from *The Nature of Christian Worship* by J. Alan Kay; the Ven. Archdeacon D. E. W. Harrison for an extract from an unpublished lecture (quoted on p. 33); Hodder & Stoughton Ltd. for two extracts from *The Spirit of Worship* by F. Heiler; the Independent Press for extracts from the *Report of the Commission on the Sacraments of Baptism and the Lord's Supper* (Congregational Union) and from *The Church and the Sacraments* by P. T. Forsyth; Messrs. Marshall, Morgan & Scott Ltd. for extracts from *The Book of Common Prayer* by D. E. W. Harrison; James Nisbet & Co. Ltd., for an extract from *Worship* by Evelyn Underhill; the Oxford University Press, London, for extracts from *An Outline of Christian Worship* and *Concerning Worship,* both by W. D. Maxwell, and from *A Book of Public Worship* compiled by John Huxtable, John Marsh, Romilly Micklem and James Todd; Charles Scribner's Sons for an extract from *Church Music in History and Practice* by W. Douglas; the S.C.M. Press Ltd. for extracts from *Ways of Worship,* a report of the Faith and Order Commission, and from *Preface to Bible Study* by Alan Richardson; Sheed & Ward Ltd. for an extract from *The Confessions of St. Augustine* translated by F. J. Sheed; the Society for Promoting Christian Knowledge for an extract from the essay by Charles Smyth in *The Genius of the Church of England* by A. E. J. Rawlinson and Charles Smyth, and for extracts from *The Background of the Prayer Book* by C. S. Phillips; the United Church of Canada for a prayer from *The Book of Common Order of the United Church of Canada.*

Prayers taken from *The Book of Common Order of the Church of Scotland* are reprinted by permission of the Committee on Public Worship and Aids to Devotion of the Church of Scotland.

CONTENTS

	PREFACE	vii
	ACKNOWLEDGEMENTS	xi
I	BASIC PRINCIPLES	1
II	ORIGINS AND DEVELOPMENT	15
III	THE MINISTRY OF THE WORD	45
IV	PUBLIC PRAYER	85
V	CHURCH PRAISE	117
VI	THE SACRAMENTS	138
	BOOKS FOR FURTHER READING	188
	INDEX	191

CHAPTER I

Basic Principles

WHAT is worship? Why do we address the chief citizen as 'His Worship the Mayor'? What exactly do we mean when we say that a man 'worships' his money—or his wife? The word is derived from the Anglo-Saxon 'weorthscipe' which became 'worthship' and then 'worship.' It means 'to ascribe worth'. Thus the title 'His Worship' signifies that we regard the chief citizen as being worthy of special honour. To say that a man 'worships' his wife means that he deems her worthy of his attentions and his love. The same is true of worship in the sense of Divine Worship. To worship God is to ascribe to Him supreme worth. It is, in the words of the Psalmist, to 'give unto the Lord the glory due unto His name' (Ps. xxix. 2).

It follows that 'worship is the only sufficient evidence of living religion.'[1] *Habere Deum est colere Deum*, said Luther[2]—if you have a God, you must of necessity worship Him. To believe in GOD—'that than which nothing greater can be conceived,' to use Anselm's phrase—implies an acknowledgement of His infinite worth. The man who says in sincerity, 'O God, thou art my God,' will also have to say, 'Worthy art thou, O Lord, to receive glory and honour and power.' If prayer is the only adequate confession of faith,

[1] J. S. Whale, *What is a Living Church?* p. 41.
[2] *Tischreden* (Kroker's ed. 1903), n. 438.

as Julius Wellhausen says, then worship is the necessary expression of faith.[1]

But how is this recognition of God's absolute worth to be expressed? It is expressed essentially in the same way in which worth in general is expressed—through an offering. The man who 'worships' his wife expresses his sense of her worth when he gives a hand with the household chores and buys her flowers. These two things—his service and his gift—constitute an offering that he makes to his wife as an acknowledgement of her worth. Now the infinite, absolute worth which we ascribe to God is expressed in essentially the same way through an offering which we bring to Him. 'Give unto the Lord the glory due unto His name,' says the psalmist; and he completes the couplet by adding, '*bring an offering,* and come into His courts' (Ps. xcvi. 8).

Hebrew worship in Old Testament times is described in one word—sacrifice. The Israelite brought to the appointed place some prescribed gift, a sheep or an ox. It must be a flawless gift, and the greater its value the more it expressed his recognition of God's supreme worth. David on one occasion refused to accept sacrificial animals from one of his subjects without payment, protesting 'neither will I offer burnt offerings unto the Lord my God of that which doth cost me nothing' (2 Sam. xxiv. 24). Hebrew sacrifice thus provided, among other things, a means of approach to God through an offering brought by the worshipper in recognition of Jehovah's worth. Taught by the prophets, however, the ancient People of God came to realize that their sacrificial gifts were not sufficient in themselves; they were intended as the outward and visible sign of an inward attitude

[1] Cf. The Report of the Faith and Order Commission, *Ways of Worship,* p. 24: 'Worship is the living form of faith.'

of mind and spirit. They were but the vehicle of the worshipper's penitence and submission, his prayer and his praise. These were the only adequate expression of his sense of God's worth. There is therefore no incongruity in the placing together, as in some of the later psalms, of sacrificial and 'spiritual' worship; the one is the visible and material expression of the other.

The subject with which we are concerned, however, is not worship in general but Christian worship—the worship by the Christian Church of God as revealed in Jesus Christ. In this worship animal sacrifice has no place; it has been superseded and 'fulfilled' in the Cross of Christ, of which it was an adumbration.[1] Christ, the Representative of a New Humanity, has offered to God, on behalf of all men, 'a full, perfect, and sufficient sacrifice' and we come to God through Him. The offering that Christians bring is what the Epistle to the Hebrews calls 'the sacrifice of praise . . ., that is, the fruit of our lips giving thanks to his name' (Heb. xiii. 15).

All that we do in Public Worship is a contribution to this offering that we bring. In our prayers we offer to God our adoration and penitence, our petitions and thanksgiving. The characteristic of the true hymn is praise to God—a note struck in the *Te Deum* and echoing in Martin Luther and Philip Doddridge, Charles Wesley and James Montgomery, John Henry Newman and Isaac Watts. The anthem sung by the choir is to the same end. The Scripture Lesson and the Sermon contribute to the same purpose, as do also the Gospel Sacraments of Holy Baptism and Holy Communion: they set forth in word and action the mighty acts of God, what He has done for us men and for our

[1] See Vincent Taylor, *Jesus and His Sacrifice,* and F. C. N. Hicks, *The Fulness of Sacrifice.*

salvation, and so evoke adoration and penitence, thanksgiving and praise.

The material gift, too, still has a place in the worship of the Christian Church. The water in the baptismal font and the bread and wine on the Lord's Table are offered to God to be the vehicles of His sacramental grace. And the offering of our gifts of money in the collection plate is no less an act of worship than are the hymns and prayers. It is the offering of our substance, the symbols of our toil and God's blessing, as a recognition that all we have comes from God. It has also a still deeper significance: it is the token and symbol of another offering which Christians make—the offering of ourselves. Here is the climax of all true worship. In response to the self-offering of God in Christ for us, we offer our praise, our prayers, our gifts; but with the realization that all these are inadequate to express the supreme worth of Him who has created us, and redeemed us, and brought us to this hour. And so we offer the greatest gift that we can bring—the gift of ourselves (Rom. xii. 1).

No gifts have we to offer
For all Thy love imparts,
But that which Thou desirest,
Our humble, thankful hearts.

Therefore, in the words of the great Eucharistic Prayer, 'here we offer and present unto thee, O Lord, ourselves, our souls and bodies, to be a reasonable, holy, and living sacrifice unto thee. . . . And although we be unworthy, through our manifold sins, to offer unto thee any sacrifice, yet we beseech thee to accept this our bounden duty and service; not weighing our merits, but pardoning our offences.'

1 REVELATION AND RESPONSE

The basis of Christian worship is not utilitarian but theological. Its practical expression therefore is controlled by certain fundamental principles which we must now consider. The first of these is that worship depends upon revelation, and Christian worship depends upon the revelation of God in Jesus Christ. Worship, that is to say, begins not from our end but from God's; it springs from the divine initiative in redemption. We come to God because God, in Jesus Christ, has come to us: we love Him because He first loved us: we ascribe to Him supreme worth because He has showed Himself to be worthy of our complete homage, gratitude and trust. Worship is essentially a response, man's response to God's Word of grace, to what He has done for us men and for our salvation.

Christianity is an historical religion. It is not a system of ideas based upon philosophical speculation or even upon observation of the natural order; it is rooted in history. In this it differs from other great world faiths. Hinduism and Buddhism find God through nature; Confucianism finds God through conduct; Christianity, and Judaism of which it is the child, find God in history. God is known for what He is by what He does. He has revealed Himself through a series of events in the life of a particular people, the Hebrews. His Word, uttered in these events, is declared by the prophets and becomes incarnate in Jesus Christ. To this Word, this self-disclosure of God, worship is the Church's response.

It follows therefore that there must be at the very heart of Christian worship a setting forth of these great saving acts of God by which He has made Himself known to men, culminating in the Incarnation, the Cross and the Resurrection. If worship is essentially a response to God's Word, that Word must be proclaimed before the response of the worshipper can be called forth. In the New Testament, as Archdeacon Harrison points out,[1] prayer and praise spring from contemplation of the saving acts of God in Jesus Christ. Eph. i. 15-22, for example, is St. Paul's response to the grace of God which is praised in verses 1-14. Similarly, the First Epistle of Peter begins by blessing God for what He has done, and the rest of the Epistle is the Christian response to this.

Thus worship, to be Christian, must embody and set forth before the eyes of the worshipper the great historic facts of the Christian revelation so that the worshipping Church may respond in penitence and thanksgiving, dedication and praise.

Every full act of Christian worship is a dramatic re-presentation of the great themes of the Christian story. The Old Testament lesson tells of the days of preparation in Israel, and the New Testament reading of the years of Christ's life, or its sequel in the Church; the breaking of bread and the pouring out of the wine take us back as no words can to the Last Supper, and to the Cross; our sharing in the bread and wine tells us that by his resurrection from the dead Christ abides with his own until the end of the world, and points forward to the time when he shall drink of the fruit of the vine new in the kingdom of God. The Sermon seeks to do what the simple rite of the Lord's Table does in action—take us back to that place where we learn anew what God has done to redeem us from sin and death, but so to take us back as to make us know that the same God is still active in the same way in the same

[1] See D. E. W. Harrison, *The Book of Common Prayer,* ch. i, to whom I am deeply indebted in this chapter.

world to save the same sinful race of men. Christian worship 'contemporizes' the Gospel.[1]

II WORSHIP IN SPIRIT

The second basic liturgical principle is that true worship can only spring from the activity of the Holy Spirit. Worship, like saving faith, is 'man's response to the nature and action of God.'[2] But the response of worship, like the response of faith, is itself the gift of God.[3] It is evoked, as we have seen, by the setting forth in word and action of the saving acts of God in human history; but it is not evoked inevitably or in any mechanistic way. No re-presentation of God's saving acts will in fact draw forth the response of real worship unless their truth 'comes home' to men and women; and that can only happen through what the Reformers called 'the inward testimony of the Holy Spirit.' The prompting of the Spirit, as the New Testament insists, is the fount of all true prayer. St. Paul reminds us that 'we know not what we should pray for as we ought: but the Spirit itself maketh intercession for us with groanings which cannot be uttered' (Rom. viii. 26). St. John's Gospel speaks of the Comforter[4] who assists the believer (Jn. xiv-xvi); the Epistle to the Hebrews portrays the Great High Priest who ever liveth to make intercession for us (Heb. vii. 25).

The conviction that true worship arises from the prompting of the Holy Spirit was the ground of the objection of the extreme left wing of the Puritan Movement to all set

[1] John Marsh, in *A Book of Public Worship*, Introduction, p. ix.

[2] J. A. Kay, *The Nature of Christian Worship*, p. 7.

[3] See Eph. ii. 8.

[4] *Paraklētos* = one called alongside to give assistance—e.g. an advocate at the Bar.

liturgical forms. The Spirit, it was argued, is the Spirit of liberty: like the wind, it bloweth where it listeth: true worship must therefore be the *ex tempore* response to the movement of the Spirit in the worshippers' hearts. Hence the use of any liturgical form was regarded as a quenching of the Spirit.

There is a considerable element of truth in this objection, as the English Free Churches have always recognized. And it has been increasingly admitted during recent years by discerning members of the Anglican Communion.[1] When worship is so restricted by liturgical forms that there is no place for free charismatic expression, it is inevitably impoverished. But there is another side of the question which is frequently overlooked by Free Churchmen: the Spirit-prompted nature of worship implies not only liberty but also an element of constraint. The Spirit is the Spirit of Christ; His function is to testify to Christ: He takes of the things of Christ and shows them unto us.[2] Worship therefore which is truly prompted by the Spirit will be subject to a theological constraint; it will be restricted as well as evoked by the Christian revelation.[3] Furthermore, since the Spirit is the Spirit of truth, which is eternal and not self-contradictory, such worship will be in line with that of Christians of past days which is crystallized in the classic liturgies of the

[1] Cf. the rubric of the 1928 Prayer Book at the end of the Occasional Prayers and Thanksgivings: 'Note, that subject to any direction which the Bishop may give, the Minister may, at his discretion, after the conclusion of Morning or Evening Prayer or of any Service contained in this Book, offer prayer in his own words.'

[2] See Jn. xiv-xvi.

[3] Cf. *Ways of Worship*, p. 19. In the more traditional forms of 'free' worship, 'this freedom is rigorously controlled by the knowledge of Scripture, the words and thoughts of which are the field in which freedom to move is given.'

Church. In so far, therefore, as a liturgy is shaped by the Christian revelation and embodies the Spirit-prompted worship of former days, it may well be the channel of the same Holy Spirit's activity in the Church today.[1] The reality of worship depends, not upon the presence or absence of a liturgy, but upon the union of the worshippers, through the power of the Spirit, with the self-oblation of Christ.

Our Lord's words to the Samaritan woman epitomize these first two basic principles of Christian worship: 'God is Spirit: and they that worship him must worship him in spirit and in truth' (Jn. iv. 24). Worship in spirit and in truth means worship, under the direction and constraint of the Spirit, of the true God[2]—God as He has revealed Himself through His saving acts recorded in the Bible, and supremely in Him who is the way, the truth and the life. The Spirit, says Jesus, 'shall take of mine and show it unto you' (Jn. xvi. 14).[3]

III WORSHIP ESSENTIALLY CORPORATE

The third fundamental principle of Christian worship is that it is essentially a corporate activity; it is the act not of isolated individuals but of the whole Church. There has

1 Cf. D. D. Williams, *Interpreting Theology, 1918-1952,* p. 36: 'Art and liturgy are the dramatic emotion-laden ways in which the message which Theology interprets finds a universal language in each generation.'

2 *alētheia* in the Fourth Gospel has a revelatory content.

3 In the Consecration Prayer of the Apostolic Constitutions, Book viii, which is based upon that of Hippolytus, God is asked 'to send His Holy Spirit upon this oblation . . . and to *show* this bread (to be) the Body of Thy Christ and the Cup His Blood.' As F. Gavin comments, 'Hippolytus is apparently dynamic; Apostolic Constitutions viii sees in the Eucharist primarily a Mystery revealed.' See 'The Eucharist in East and West' in *Liturgy and Worship* (ed. Clarke and Harris), pp. 118-19.

been an increasing recognition of this fact during recent years: 'There is a growing sense that worship is not to be thought of as a gathering of individual pious Christians, but as a corporate act in direct relation to the Lord of the Church.'[1] This is not to deny the validity, or the necessity, of private devotion; it is rather to see it in the proper perspective. 'There is a side of our religious life which is intimately private, a secret between our souls and God; but there are times when we want to forget ourselves in a larger whole: it is to this need that worship ministers, directing our minds towards the Glory of God and the welfare of His Church.'[2] The Christian's private approach to God is on the ground of his union with Christ. But to be 'in Christ' means to be incorporated into His Body which is the obedient, worshipping Church. Hence 'private worship is based on corporate worship, the worship of the Church, the Body of the Lord.'[3] Christian worship is the corporate approach to God of the People of God. It is a family activity. 'When ye pray,' said Jesus, 'say, *Our* Father. . . .'

This principle is a corollary of the New Testament doctrine of the priesthood of all believers, so dear to Reformed Churchmen. Christians—all Christians—constitute a 'kingdom of priests.' This means, however, not only that every Christian has direct access to the Presence of God through the one Mediator, Jesus Christ; it has another implication which is frequently overlooked. The function of a priest is to offer a sacrifice; that is his *raison d'être*. If then Christians form a 'kingdom of priests,' as the New Testament

[1] *Ways of Worship,* p. 20.

[2] F. H. Brabant, 'Worship in General' in *Liturgy and Worship* (ed. Clarke and Harris), p. 37.

[3] *Ways of Worship,* p. 25.

declares,[1] it follows that their function as a corporate whole is to make an offering to God; they are to offer the sacrifice of praise continually and themselves as a reasonable, holy, and living sacrifice. In other words, one of the chief functions of the Church, part of its *raison d'être,* is the offering of its corporate worship to God. In this the Church, like the priest, acts vicariously: it offers to God, on behalf of humanity, what He requires of all men by giving unto the Lord the glory due unto His Name. This is expressed in St. Paul's transformation of the priestly terms of the Old Testament into the priestliness of the Gospel. 'That I might be the priest (*leitourgos*) of Jesus Christ to the Gentiles, sacrificing (*hierourgounta*) the gospel of God, that the sacrificial offering (*prosphora*) of the Gentiles might be acceptable, being sanctified by the Holy Spirit' (Rom. xv. 16).

There is another aspect of the corporateness of Christian worship: it is the worship of the *whole* Church, militant on earth and triumphant in heaven. On the walls of a Greek Orthodox Church there are pictures of the saints—'ikons,' as they are called. Their purpose is to recall to the worshipper that the Church consists not merely of the local congregation, or even of the sum-total of local congregations; it consists also of believers of past days, the great multitude of the redeemed gathered with the heavenly host around the throne of God. And when the deacon, by censing the ikons, greets the 'guests come to the sacramental feast,'[2] the worshipper is reminded that in his worship he is united in the communion of saints with the worship of the whole Church, in heaven as well as on earth.

During the First World War the regiment of a cynical

[1] 1 Pet. ii. 5 and 9; Rev. i. 6, v. 10.

[2] N. B. Gogol, *Meditations on the Divine Liturgy,* p. 21.

English colonel was billeted in a French village. Nothing delighted the colonel more than the opportunity of taking a rise out of the old village priest. One Sunday morning he passed the church as a handful of people were leaving Mass. 'Good morning, Father,' he said to the priest at the door. 'Not very many at Mass this morning, Father—not very many!' 'No, my son, you're wrong,' was the reply. 'Thousands and thousands and tens of thousands!'

Therefore with angels and archangels, and with all the company of heaven, we laud and magnify thy glorious Name; evermore praising thee, and saying: Holy, holy, holy, Lord God of hosts, heaven and earth are full of thy glory: Glory be to thee, O Lord most high.

IV WORSHIP AND WITNESS

One final principle remains to be considered: worship is the only adequate preparation of the Church for its work and witness in the world as the Body of Christ. As E. R. Micklem reminds us, 'in order that she shall accomplish anything the Church must live, and her life depends on her worship.'[1] That is not to say that worship is to be regarded as a means to an end. It is an end in itself; in it man achieves his chief end of glorifying God. There is no greater human activity than that of giving unto the Lord the glory due unto His name. Hence, for Christians the obligation of worship is absolute and any merely subjective evaluation of it is misleading.

At the close of a series of sermons on worship, the writer was approached by a very sincere young man. 'Do you think I ought to come to church when I don't feel like it?' he asked. 'There are times when I want to come and really

[1] *Our Approach to God,* p. 11.

enjoy the service, but there are other times when I've no inclination at all. Wouldn't it be hypocritical to come then?' 'Well, John,' I replied, 'do you only pay the grocer's bill and the rent when you feel like it?' He saw the point at once. Worship is a debt to be discharged independently of our feelings; it is giving unto the Lord the glory *due* unto His name; hence 'it is obligatory on Christians.'[1] The primary purpose of worship is the glory of God, not the edification of man; 'God must come first, or man's edification will not follow.'[2]

Man's edification does follow, however, when worship is directed to its proper end. 'What we become in the presence of God,' says a German mystic, 'that we can be all day long.'[3] It is through worship that the Church is united by the Holy Spirit to Christ in His self-oblation to the Father, and hence becomes the instrument of His saving activity in the world. The measure of the Church's power is the measure of her union with her Lord. It is as the Body of Christ, indwelt by His Spirit and reflecting His glory, that the People of God fulfil their vocation in the world. In a word, effective witness depends upon sustained worship. 'What matters,' says Archdeacon Harrison, 'is not whether worship makes us feel good or happy; what matters is whether it makes us Christ-like; whether men take knowledge of us that we have been with Jesus.'[4]

The Exhortation at the beginning of Mattins in the Book of Common Prayer contains a brief but pregnant summary of the purpose of Christian worship. We assemble and meet together in the presence of God

[1] F. H. Brabant in *Liturgy and Worship,* p. 31.

[2] *Ways of Worship,* p. 33.

[3] Quoted by D. E. W. Harrison, op. cit., p. 19.

[4] ibid., p. 20.

to render thanks for the great benefits that we have received at his hands, to set forth his most worthy praise, to hear his most holy Word, and to ask those things which are requisite and necessary, as well for the body as the soul.

These central elements—the Ministry of the Word, Prayer, and Praise, will engage our attention in the following chapters. First, however, we must endeavour to see present-day worship against the background of its historical development. To this we now turn.

CHAPTER II

Origins and Development

I THE EUCHARISTIC NORM

THE first Christians were Jews, brought up from childhood in the worship of the Synagogue. This consisted of the reading and exposition of the Law in a setting of prayer and praise. The Prophetic Books were read as a commentary on the Law, the psalms were sung as acts of praise, and the form of the prayers had become fixed so that all could take part in them. This was the kind of worship in which our Lord and His Apostles shared each Sabbath day. When therefore Christians were expelled from the synagogues they naturally shaped their own worship along these familiar lines. Their emphasis, however, moved from the Law to the Prophetic Books, which they reinterpreted in the light of Christ, and in course of time their own scriptures were added and came to occupy the chief place.

But this was not the whole of early Christian worship; to it was added another element given by our Lord Himself in the Upper Room—the rite of 'the breaking of bread.' 'More than words could do, this holy action brought to mind all that our Lord had done, and made them supremely conscious of His living Presence with them.'[1]

It is clear from the Acts of the Apostles that these two elements were inseparably united in the worship of the Apostolic Church. 'They continued steadfastly in the apostles' doctrine and fellowship, and in breaking of bread,

[1] W. D. Maxwell, *An Outline of Christian Worship*, p. 4.

and in prayers' (Acts ii. 42). 'And upon the first day of the week, when the disciples came together to break bread, Paul preached unto them' (Acts xx. 7). In other words, the gathering of Christians for worship each Lord's Day was a Eucharist in which prayer and praise and instruction in righteousness were united indivisibly with the sacramental fellowship of the Lord's Supper. We may infer from 1 Cor. xi that this was certainly the practice of the Church at Corinth. The 'breaking of bread' was then part of a common meal, the *agapē;* but this latter was soon separated from the Eucharist proper and eventually disappeared from the life of the Church leaving only the ceremonial meal.

> Thus [says Maxwell] Christian worship, as a distinctive, indigenous thing, arose from the fusion, in the crucible of Christian experience, of the Synagogue and the Upper Room. Thus fused, each completing and quickening the other, they became the norm of Christian worship. Christian worship found other forms of expression, but these belong to the circumference, not to the centre. The typical worship of the Church is to be found to this day in the union of the worship of the Synagogue and the sacramental experience of the Upper Room; and that union dates from New Testament times.[1]

A graphic picture of second-century worship at Rome, showing the blending of these same two elements, is given by Justin Martyr in his *First Apology* to the Emperor Antoninus Pius (c.140):

> On the day called the Feast of the Sun, all who live in towns or in the country assemble in one place, and the memoirs of the Apostles or the writings of the Prophets are read as time permits. Then, when the reader has ended, the President instructs and encourages the people to practise the truths contained in the Scripture lections. Thereafter, we all stand up

[1] op. cit., p. 5.

and offer prayers together; and, as I mentioned before, when we have concluded this prayer, bread and wine and water are brought.

Then the President likewise offers up prayers and thanksgivings according to his ability, and the people cry aloud saying Amen. Each one then receives a portion and share of the elements over which thanks have been given; and which are also carried and ministered by the deacons to those absent.[1]

Here again we have a Eucharistic service in which prayer, reading and instruction are united with, and find their climax in, the ceremony of the bread and wine. As Maxwell points out, 'In this early worship it will be observed that the balance was kept between the sacramental and Scriptural elements: both the reading of the Scriptures with instruction and the consecration and reception of the bread and wine were integral parts of the rite. Without either it was incomplete.'[2]

From this fluid worship of the Primitive Church there developed the distinctive Eastern and Western rites. The basic structure of both was the same, consisting of the two essential elements of Word and Sacrament, but each developed a distinctive character and emphasis. In the East there grew up an elaborate ceremonial, rich in symbolism, which is lacking in the briefer and more direct Western rite. The East, for example, transferred the preparation of the elements to a service of Prothesis, symbolizing the details of the Passion, with which the worship begins; the West retained the original order beginning with the Liturgy of the Word.

'In the East the notion of mystery is dominant, and tends

[1] See *First Apology,* lxv-lxvii. [2] op. cit., p. 13.

more and more to absorb the whole worship into itself.'[1] The action of the Sacrament is hidden from the worshippers by a screen, the Ikonostasis, the doors of which are closed during the Liturgy of the Upper Room. There are two ceremonial entrances through the Royal Door into the Sanctuary—the 'Little Entrance' of the celebrant and a deacon, carrying the book of the Gospels, during the Liturgy of the Word; and the 'Great Entrance' in which, after the Prayers of the Faithful in the Liturgy of the Upper Room, the elements prepared in the service of Prothesis are brought to the Lord's Table.

More important are the distinctive theological emphases of the Eastern and Western rites which spring from the differing conceptions of salvation which underlie them. For the East salvation is the deification of humanity through the Incarnation; for the West it results from the propitiatory sacrifice of the Cross. The Eastern Eucharist is therefore an act of communion, while in the West the idea of propitiatory sacrifice is dominant. 'In the Eastern rite what is offered is the gifts of the worshippers to be consecrated by the Spirit for sacramental use, whereas in the Mass it is the body and blood of Christ that are offered as a sacrifice after the consecration has taken place.'[2]

Along with this Eastern elaboration of ceremonial and Western perversion of the primitive rite we find in both East and West a decline in preaching during the Middle Ages, the Eucharist being frequently celebrated with no sermon at all. As a result the original balance of Word and Sacrament was lost. Worship in the East became virtually

1 R. S. Franks, 'Christian Worship in the Middle Ages' in *Christian Worship* (ed. N. Micklem), p. 112.

2 R. S. Franks, op. cit., p. 115.

the enactment of a mystery-rite and in the West a spectacular drama culminating in the miracle of transubstantiation. Nevertheless, as Franks reminds us, 'the very first point to be observed about Medieval Christianity both in East and West is that the Eucharist remains as it was in the Ancient Church the fundamental and central Christian service, to which everything else leads up and in relation to which all else is to be interpreted.'[1]

II THE QUIRE OFFICES

Around this central act of Christian worship, known in the Middle Ages as the Mass, there grew up a series of supplementary daily services, the Hours of prayer, which were observed as the chief duty (*officium*) of the monastic orders and hence known as Offices. Since they were said, or sung, in the quire of the church or abbey, they have come to be called the Quire[2] Offices.

Their origin is obscure, but they seem to have been derived from the private devotions and family prayers of the early Christians. The Apostles and their followers observed the Jewish hours of prayer, indications of which are found in the Old Testament. Daniel is said to have prayed three times a day (Dan. vi. 10); Psalm lv mentions evening, morning and noon as hours of prayer (ver. 17); another psalmist speaks of seven daily occasions (Ps. cxix. 164) and refers to midnight as one of them (ver. 62). In the New

[1] ibid., p. 109.

[2] Sometimes spelt 'Choir.' Here 'choir' is used to indicate the body of singers and 'quire' the place of the singers.

Testament the third, sixth and ninth hours[1] (i.e. 9.0 a.m., noon and 3.0 p.m.) are specifically mentioned. The descent of the Holy Spirit on the day of Pentecost takes place as the disciples are gathered together at the third hour (Acts ii. 1 and 15). St. Peter's vision is given as he prays on the housetop at the sixth hour (Acts iii. 9). St. Peter and St. John go into the Temple at the ninth hour (Acts iii. 1) and it was as he prayed at this same hour that Cornelius received his vision (Acts x. 3 and 30). Later patristic writings make frequent reference to these hours[2] and it is clear that Christians also prayed on rising in the morning and retiring at night. Indeed a devotional manual issued for converts in Rome in the early third century makes it obligatory for Christians to pray six times a day—on rising, at the third, sixth and ninth hours, on going to bed, and in the middle of the night.[3]

The reference so far is still only to private prayer and no form for this is prescribed. Once this stage was reached, however, the transition from free private prayers to ordered public prayers at the same fixed hours was easily made. As Ratcliffe observes, 'Common prayer at stated times in church is the next step to obligatory private prayer at the same times at home' and 'there is, also, but a short distance between direction to say prayers, and direction as to what prayers to say.'[4] Thus we find daily public services at six

1 There is clearly a reference to the Passion: 'It was the third hour, and they crucified him' (Mk. xv. 25). 'And when the sixth hour was come, there was darkness over the whole land until the ninth hour. And at the ninth hour Jesus cried with a loud voice. . . .' (Mk. xv. 33-34).

2 Their observance is mentioned by Clement, Origen, Tertullian and Cyprian.

3 *Apostolic Tradition* of Hippolytus (c.235).

4 E. C. Ratcliffe, 'The Choir Offices' in *Liturgy and Worship*, p. 259.

fixed hours in general use at the end of the fourth century. Morning and evening were the principal times and for these psalms and prayers were prescribed.[1]

It was in the monasteries, however, that the daily Offices assumed their final definite structure and content through the formulation of the Benedictine Rule (c.530). St. Benedict adapted the Roman public services for monastic use and to the six Roman Offices he added a dawn Office, Prime, and a late evening Office, Compline.[2] The final order of the Canonical Hours, as they came to be called, was thus: Vigils or Nocturns (later called Mattins) at about 2 a.m., Lauds at daybreak, Prime in the early morning, Terce at 9 a.m., Sext at noon, None 2-3 p.m., Vespers about 6 p.m., and Compline about 8 p.m. In practice Mattins and Lauds were said together as a single service, thus reducing the number of Offices to seven in accordance with Ps. cxix. 164: 'Seven times a day do I praise thee.' The daily Mass was said before Sext. The late Middle Ages saw a further modification of practice: it became customary, for the sake of convenience, to say the Offices in the parish, as distinct from the monastic, churches in two groups, the first four being said together in the morning and the remaining four in the evening. The significance of this will be seen when we consider the liturgical developments of the English Reformation.

The Canonical Hours were an ellipse with two foci—the orderly recitation of the Psalter once a week and the consecutive reading of Holy Scripture, the Old Testament being read through once a year and the New Testament twice.

[1] See the *Apostolic Constitutions* (c.375-400).

[2] Prime and Compline were taken by St. Benedict from the Rule of St. Basil.

C. S. Phillips gives a clear and concise summary of their structure and content:

The night-Office called Mattins had a form of its own, and provided for the greater part of the weekly recitation of the Psalter and the whole of the consecutive reading of Scripture. . . . The psalms were preceded by the *Venite,* and on festivals *Te Deum* was sung at the end. Of the other services Lauds and Vespers were similar in structure. In each case the service consisted of the recitation of psalms—fixed at Lauds (including the 'praise-psalms' cxlviii-cl), and varying at Vespers; a short 'chapter'[1] of Scripture (varying); an Office Hymn (varying); a fixed Canticle (*Benedictus* at Lauds, *Magnificat* at Vespers); and a Collect and other prayers at the end. These three were the most important services, the other five being known as the Lesser Hours. Of these Prime and Compline (i.e. the 'completing' service that closed the day) were framed on one common pattern, while Terce, Sext and None were framed on another. The latter group, along with Prime, provided for the daily recitation of Psalm cxix, which was divided into four portions for the purpose, the *Quicunque vult* following the Prime portion. All five had their hymns (fixed except at Compline), their 'chapters' and their Collects; while at Compline was sung the Canticle *Nunc dimittis.* Throughout the cycle the psalms and canticles were provided with antiphons; and each service began with introductory versicles that still survive in our own Prayer Book.[2]

With the possible exception of Mattins, therefore, the emphasis of the Divine Office[3] was praise and prayer rather than edification.

III REFORMATION DEVELOPMENTS

At the close of the Middle Ages worship in the West was

[1] These *capitula* or 'chapters' consisted of a single verse.
[2] *The Background of the Prayer Book,* pp. 91-2.
[3] The cycle of Hours, which was the chief duty (*officium*) of the monastics, was known as the *Opus Dei*—the 'work' or 'service' of God. Hence the term 'Divine Office.'

virtually the preserve of clergy and monks. The Daily Offices had been collected together into a single book called the Breviary; another book, the Missal, contained the Mass. Both were in Latin—an academic tongue since the fall of the Roman Empire. This, together with the decline in preaching, resulted in the virtual disappearance of edification from the worship of ordinary people. Their own active participation, apart from 'adoration, not unmixed with superstition'[1] at the elevation of the consecrated elements in the Mass, was confined to communicating, in the bread only, once a year at Easter. The great central rite of Christendom had become a drama performed by the clergy in an unknown tongue,[2] a spectacle to be witnessed, but no longer a corporate act of worship.

In a letter of Stephen Gardiner to Cranmer written in July 1547[3] the standpoint of the late medieval churchman is bluntly stated:

> For in times past . . . the people in the church took small heed what the priest and the clerks did in the chancel, but only to stand up at the Gospel and kneel at the Sacring, or else every man was occupied himself severally in several prayer. . . . It was never meant that the people should indeed hear the Mattins or hear the Mass, but be present there and pray themselves in silence; with common credit to the priests and clerks, that although they hear not a distinct sound to know what they say, yet to judge that they for their part were and be

1 W. D. Maxwell, op. cit., p. 72.

2 A short service in the vernacular, known as the Prone, was sometimes inserted into the Mass. It consisted of bidding prayers, the Epistle and Gospel, the Creed, the sermon (if any), exhortation, and the Lord's Prayer or a paraphrase of it. It was not, however, a part of the authorized text of the Mass. The Prone was very popular. In England it was known as The Bidding of the Bedes.

3 Quoted by Charles Smyth in *The Genius of the Church of England*.

well occupied, and in prayer; and so should they be. . . . Thus it hath been practised.

And thus Gardiner, for his part, wanted it to continue. 'But Cranmer,' comments Canon Smyth, 'knew from the New Testament that it *was* meant that the congregation should understand and follow and take part in the drama of the Eucharist, and that the primary purpose for which the Supper of the Lord was instituted was not adoration, but communion: and on both counts he has been vindicated by the modern Liturgical Reform Movement in the Church of Rome.' The Pope's injunction, 'You are not to pray *at* the Mass, you are to pray the Mass,' is 'a belated echo of the principles of the English Reformation.'[1]

All the Reformers, with the exception of Zwingli,[2] attempted to restore the original Eucharist, in which the preaching of the Word culminated in the communion of the worshippers at the Table of the Lord, as the weekly norm of worship. Using Holy Scripture as their criterion, they repudiated the unscriptural notion of transubstantiation and stripped away the medieval accretions which obscured the essential elements of the rite. To quote J. S. Whale's telling epigram, 'Reformers are iconoclasts only because Catholics have been innovators.'[3] The Mass, which was independent of the participation of the worshippers, became once more the Lord's Supper with its climax, not in the consecration and oblation of the elements, but in the communion of the people.

[1] *The Genius of the Church of England*, p. 30.

[2] Zwingli, for whom the Lord's Supper was primarily a confessional act, desired its celebration only four times a year—at Easter, Pentecost, Harvest and Christmas.

[3] 'Calvin' in *Christian Worship* (Ed. N. Micklem), p. 161.

There is, moreover, a complete change of emphasis in Protestant worship. In contrast to the medieval liturgies of both East and West, in which the Sacramental Act predominates to the virtual exclusion of the Ministry of the Word, 'the Reformation laid primary emphasis on the Word as the basis of faith and worship.'[1] The Word is not an insertion, like the Prone, into an otherwise complete sacramental drama; the Sacrament itself is a seal of the Word. Thus, 'two facts dominate Protestant worship. First, the central place given to the sermon; second, the transformation of the Mass into the Communion of the Lord's Supper.'[2]

Because they regarded the Word as being of primary importance, the Reformers insisted that worship be rational and intelligible. The use of the vernacular is thus a feature common to all branches of Protestantism. The service must be in a language 'understanded of the people.' Moreover, the minister conducting it must so stand that he can be clearly heard and his actions at the Holy Table seen. He stands therefore behind the Communion Table, facing the people, as was the custom in the early Church.[3] The people too take their own distinctive part through the congregational singing of hymns or metrical psalms, an innovation introduced by Luther and Calvin. 'The great point of difference between the medieval and the modern hymn,'

[1] J. S. Whale, op. cit., p. 165.

[2] ibid., pp. 166-7.

[3] This was the position taken by the bishop in the apse of the early basilicas, hence known as the 'basilican posture.' Luther, while advocating it in the introduction to his *Deutsche Messe,* seems himself to have continued to celebrate in the eastward position. It was adopted, however, by Calvin and became general in the Reformed Churches.

Whale reminds us, 'lies in the fact that the former was monastic, belonging almost exclusively to the clerks in the choir . . . the latter belongs to the people. . . . If there is any Protestant counterpart of the medieval office hymn in the Latin Breviary it is perhaps the anthem sung by the modern church-choir.'[1]

Luther, who was the most conservative of the Reformers, was slow to change anything in the Mass which was not explicitly forbidden in Holy Scripture. Indeed his *Formula Missae* of 1523, upon which most of the later Lutheran liturgies are based, 'is merely a truncated version of the Roman mass, retaining the Latin language, most of the ceremonial, lights, incense, and vestments.'[2] Three years later, however, he published his *Deutsche Messe* in the vernacular in which far-reaching and even drastic changes are made; but vestments and lights are still retained. 'As a form,' says Maxwell, 'Luther's German mass was defective in many parts. But he broadened and deepened the spirit of worship and gave the people a more intelligible part. They now knew at least what was being done, and could join in the common action; and communion was restored to its rightful place. The impetus given by Luther to the hymnody of the Church was to produce lasting and glorious benefits.'[3]

The radical Reformer was Calvin. Heiler's assertion, however, that he 'succeeded in creating a form of service in which no fragment of any importance from the Roman Mass remained,'[4] credits Calvin with too much. Calvin's service was not his own creation but an adaptation of

[1] op. cit., p. 164.

[2] W. D. Maxwell, op. cit., p. 77.

[3] ibid., p. 80.

[4] F. Heiler, *The Spirit of Worship*, p. 99.

Bucer's Strasbourg rite, and this at least followed the main outline of the Roman Canon. All the same, the Mass itself was for Calvin the supreme abomination set up by Satan. His sole criteria were Scripture and ancient ecclesiastical usage. Symbolism of ornament and ceremonial he regarded as unscriptural human devices detracting from the glory of God. They were therefore reduced to their simplest form. Nevertheless, as Doumergue points out, 'all the essential elements of worship were there.'[1] Calvin did not wish to replace the Mass by a preaching service, as is frequently alleged; he sought to replace the degenerate medieval Mass by a weekly Eucharist in which the primitive balance of Word and Sacrament was restored, a celebration of the Lord's Supper with sermon and communion taking their rightful place.

Calvin's ideal of a weekly Communion, however, was never realized; the opposition of the Genevan magistrates limited him to four celebrations a year.[2] But he accepted this limitation only under protest and as a provisional arrangement of which he strongly disapproved. Moreover, on the Sunday mornings when he was not permitted to celebrate the Supper, Calvin retained the structure and content of the Eucharist, omitting only those parts directly related to the consecration of the elements and communion. The eucharistic norm of worship was thus maintained. 'Calvin's service,' says Whale, 'is not derived from the medieval daily offices or choir services, nor is it parallel to Anglican Mattins,

[1] E. Doumergue, *Jean Calvin,* vol. ii, p. 504.

[2] The medieval norm of Communion once a year meant inevitably that the establishment of weekly Communion was bound to be a difficult and slow process. The Reformers' emphasis was based not only on primitive practice but also on their insistence that religion must be personal as well as corporate.

which go back through the seven daily offices to the Benedictine Rule. . . . Just as the famous Confession of Sins springs from the Confiteor of the Mass, so the Great Prayer of Intercession is derived not from medieval Bidding prayers but from the Canon. Calvin's ordinary Sunday morning service, like that of John Knox, was thus a classical Ante-Communion.'[1]

The English Reformation was unique; it followed no precedents but attempted to steer a middle course between the Scylla of Rome and the Charybdis of Geneva. This has given to the Anglican Church that mixed character which it has always retained, a source of both its weakness and its strength. Thus, while its doctrine as crystallized in the Articles of Religion is Calvinistic to the core, its worship is directed by a Prayer Book compiled from medieval sources. In liturgical practice it has close affinities with Lutheranism, although the influence of Calvin can be seen.[2]

The Book of Common Prayer—the only service book dating from the Reformation still in use— is a monument to the genius of Archbishop Cranmer under whose direction the First and Second Prayer Books of Edward VI (published in 1549 and 1552 respectively) took shape. One of the ablest liturgical scholars of his day, Cranmer had both a profound knowledge of the medieval heritage and a close acquaintance with leaders of the continental reforms, besides being himself a master of English style. His guiding principles are set out in the Preface of the First Prayer Book of 1549, which appears in the present 1662 Prayer Book

[1] op. cit., p. 171.

[2] E.g., the Decalogue in the Communion Office of the Second Prayer Book of 1552 is derived from Calvin's rite, as is also the penitential introduction to Morning and Evening Prayer.

under the heading, 'Concerning the Service of the Church.' The first is that 'all things shall be read and sung . . . in the English tongue, to the end that the Congregation may be thereby edified.' Secondly, the services are to be simplified since hitherto their intricacies were such that 'many times there was more business to find out what should be read, than to read it when it was found out.' Thirdly, the essential elements of the Western liturgical tradition are to be restored to their ancient place and given their proper emphasis by eliminating unprofitable accretions 'whereof some are untrue, some uncertain, some vain and superstitious.' Fourthly, 'whereas heretofore there hath been great diversity in saying and singing in Churches within this Realm . . . now from henceforth all the whole Realm shall have but one Use.' All these, except the final principle of liturgical uniformity, are common also to the continental Reformers.

In the interests of simplification, Cranmer aimed at bringing together all the chief public services of the Church into one book. The resulting First Prayer Book of Edward VI (1549) was a notable achievement. 'It represented an honest and conservative attempt to maintain the liturgical tradition of the Western Church in its really essential features.'[1] In the Eucharist, which was to be celebrated with communion every Sunday and Holy Day, 'the outline of the old Latin Mass was strictly adhered to, with all its main constituent parts presented in their accustomed order.'[2] The Canon (as the Consecration Prayer was called) was new but followed the main lines of the old Roman Canon with the addition of an invocation of the Holy Spirit (Epiclesis) as found in the ancient liturgies and preserved in the Eastern rites.

[1] C. S. Phillips, op. cit., p. 26. [2] ibid.

It was in the Divine Office that the greatest changes occurred. As we have seen, at the time of the Reformation it had become customary in parish churches to say the Canonical Hours in two groups, one in the morning and the other in the evening. This suggested to Cranmer a further simplification:

The old scheme of eight services in twenty-four hours was abandoned in favour of two services—to be said morning and evening—called 'Mattins' and 'Evensong' respectively. Of these the former represented a combination of elements drawn from the old Mattins, Lauds and Prime; the latter, framed on the same model, included elements taken from Vespers and Compline; while Terce, Sext and None disappeared altogether. . . . The traditional sequence of psalms, lessons, canticles and prayers was reproduced in a simpler and compressed form; and the essential purpose of the Divine Office—the systematic recitation of the Psalter and reading of Holy Scripture—was secured by a scheme which provided for the saying of the entire Psalter once a month (instead of once a week, as formerly in theory) and the reading of the great bulk of the Old Testament once a year and of the whole New Testament twice a year.[1]

There is, moreover, a significant change of emphasis. The Preface of the 1549 Prayer Book, as F. C. Burkitt points out, implies that 'whereas the old daily offices had their centre of gravity in the recital of the Psalms, in Cranmer's view . . . the centre is in the reading of the Bible.'[2]

Upon this first English Prayer Book all later versions are based. The book itself, however, was too conservative to be acceptable to the more thorough-going Protestants, pressure from whom resulted in the publication of the Second Prayer Book of Edward VI in 1552. Here significant changes occur

[1] C. S. Phillips, op. cit., p. 27.

[2] *Christian Worship*, p. 83.

with mixed results. On the one hand, the 1552 Prayer Book has a more definitely Protestant character that that of 1549; on the other hand, it initiates a departure from classic liturgical tradition which has characterized the Book of Common Prayer ever since. Not only were the ancient chants and other primitive features of the Communion Office omitted, but the great Consecration Prayer, or Canon, was broken up into three sections. The Intercessions with which it began were set further back in the service as the Prayer for the Church Militant, and the remaining part of the prayer was divided into two portions between which was inserted the Communion. The Lord's Prayer was moved from the end of the Canon where it had formed the climax from early times, and placed immediately after the Communion, to be followed by the Prayer of Oblation which was now made interchangeable with the post-communion prayer.[1] The invocation of the Holy Spirit (Epiclesis) disappeared altogether. Little change was made in the Offices of Morning and Evening Prayer apart from the provision of the penitential introduction.[2]

It seems that Cranmer's object in this radical rearrangement of the service of Holy Communion was to emphasize the Protestant character of the rite, both by a departure from the form of the old Roman Canon and by giving to the Communion itself a more central place, to the extent of inserting in into the heart of the Canon. On theological grounds it has been argued that self-oblation is only possible through the grace given in the reception of the consecrated

[1] In fact, therefore, there are two distinct rites in the Book of Common Prayer.

[2] In the 1549 Prayer Book the Daily Office begins with the Lord's Prayer (said as a preparation) and the versicles, 'O Lord, open thou our lips,' etc.

elements. Hence the Prayer of Oblation, with which the Canon ends, is more fittingly placed after the act of Communion. But it now becomes optional, and the fact remains that Cranmer's rearrangement breaks with the liturgical tradition not only of the medieval but also of the primitive Church.

The Prayer Books of 1559 (following the 'Catholic interlude' of Mary's reign) and 1662 (following the Commonwealth) are in structure and content virtually the same as that of 1552. The small changes made in each are in the 'Catholic' direction with the object of toning down the Protestant character of the 1552 book. For example, the Words of Administration in the First Prayer Book of Edward VI (1549) are: 'The Body of our Lord Jesus Christ, which was given for thee, preserve thy body and soul unto everlasting life.' This is Lutheran and capable of a 'Catholic' interpretation. It is therefore replaced in the 1552 Prayer Book by the Zwinglian form: 'Take and eat this in remembrance that Christ died for thee, and feed on him in thy heart by faith with thanksgiving.' But in the Prayer Books of 1559 and 1662 both forms are conflated: 'The Body of our Lord Jesus Christ, which was given for thee, preserve thy body and soul unto everlasting life: Take and eat this in remembrance that Christ died for thee, and feed on him in thy heart by faith with thanksgiving.'

The 1662 Book of Common Prayer has remained the only legally authorized form of Anglican worship in England until the present day. The Revised Prayer Book of 1927-8, which Maxwell describes as 'a praiseworthy attempt to restore the ancient unity and sequence of the English rite,'[1] was approved by Convocation, the Church Assembly

[1] op. cit., p. 151.

and the House of Lords, but controversy regarding Reservation of the Sacrament resulted in its rejection by the House of Commons. The first stage of the revision, the Revised Lectionary, had however been legalized as an alternative to the old Lectionary in 1922 and other parts of the book are authorized (although not legally) by many of the bishops for use in their own dioceses.

All the Reformers inherited from the Middle Ages a double tradition of Eucharist and Quire Offices, but it was only Cranmer who deliberately retained both. In this his liturgical genius is seen. And he not only adapts the medieval Quire Offices to the needs of Reformed parish worship; he places at their centre the reading and hearing of the Word of God.

It is important to realize that Cranmer was not primarily concerned with producing a revised breviary, a choir-office for the clergy, nor with the simple restoration of an unbroken course of psalms and lections freed from mediæval elaboration and interpolation : he was concerned with common prayer, with the needs of the whole Church, laity as well as clergy. Judged in the light of history his order for Morning and Evening Prayer is his most remarkable achievement. For, however much we may deplore the fact, when judged by our highest ideals, it is true that the influence of the Prayer Book on the great mass of English Churchmen has been primarily the influence of Mattins and Evensong, and that continuously throughout its history.[1]

Thus, by retaining and recasting the Quire Offices, Cranmer succeeded in providing a form of worship which is complementary to the Eucharist. 'The peculiarity of the Anglican tradition,' says Evelyn Underhill, 'is the equal emphasis which it gives to the Divine Office and the Eucharist;

[1] D. E. W. Harrison. Quoted from an unpublished lecture.

that is to say, to Biblical and to Sacramental worship. Where this balance is disturbed, its special character is lost. . . . The *Ecclesia Anglicana* alone—though "Protestant" and "Catholic" extremists may tend to cultivate one strand to the detriment of the rest—is true to the primitive pattern; and along both these paths leads out her people towards God.' 'This,' she goes on, 'is a fact not lightly to be set aside; for it creates a special liturgical formula, in which are united just those elements of worship most deeply valued by the English soul. The scriptural quality, the grave theocentric temper, the common singing of psalms and spiritual songs, and the dependence on Providence which is expressed in the prayers for the community and the common needs of daily life, exactly fit the Morning and Evening Prayer of the English Church to the religious temper of her children.'[1]

Cranmer does not appear to have worked out the precise relationship between the Eucharist and the Quire Offices.[2] It is clear, however, that he intended the weekly Eucharist to be the chief Sunday service—'the Lord's service for the Lord's people on the Lord's day.' Morning Prayer and the Litany are meant to precede and lead up to it, as the rubrics of 1549 and 1552 indicate.[3] Its centrality is evident from the fact that here alone in the whole of the Book of Common Prayer is there any provision for the preaching of the Word.

1 *Worship*, pp. 335-6.

2 In Cranmer's Prayer Books the Sunday lessons and psalms follow in order from the previous week. Special lessons for Sunday were an Elizabethan innovation.

3 Intending communicants are required to signify their names to the Curate overnight 'or els in the morning, afore the beginning of Matins, or immediately after.' And 'after the Letany ended' the Priest proceeds with the Communion Office (1549).

Unhappily the practice of the Church of England has become far removed from the intentions of its Prayer Book. C. S. Phillips, himself an Anglican minister, admits that in his own Church 'the Communion Office did tend more and more as time went on to fall into the background in comparison with the other services. Celebrations became less frequent, until in the dark days of the eighteenth century four or three times a year was frequently deemed sufficient. And even when it was celebrated more often, the majority of the laity showed no great eagerness to communicate.'[1] The result has been that Morning Prayer (or sometimes Evening Prayer) has largely replaced the Eucharist as the central Sunday service. In order to restore something of the fulness of worship, a sermon is now added on Sundays to Morning and Evening Prayer, the Holy Communion—without a sermon—being celebrated at an early hour and attended by only a few worshippers. This is quite contrary to the intentions of the Book of Common Prayer in which a sermon is prescribed only at the Eucharist.

IV FREE CHURCH WORSHIP

The Anglican Settlement was a compromise between Geneva and Rome; hence it was not acceptable to the radical element in the English Church. The Protestant exiles, who had been guests of the Continental Reformed Churches during Mary's reign, did not take kindly to the Prayer Book of 1559 on their return. What they regarded as 'remnants of popery' contrasted vividly with the worship according to the 'pure' Word of God to which they had

[1] C. S. Phillips, op. cit., p. 44.

become accustomed at Geneva and elsewhere. These 'Puritans,' as they were nicknamed by their opponents, ranged themselves with Calvin in their insistence that only what was expressly authorized in Scripture had any place in worship; the Anglicans maintained with Luther that only what was explicitly forbidden in Scripture need be removed.[1] For the Puritans the Genevan form of service was the model of Reformed worship, to which they desired the English Church to conform.

In the latter part of the sixteenth century there appeared within the Puritan movement two wings from which emerged two distinct Protestant groups, the Presbyterians and the Independents. The Presbyterians, although dissatisfied with the Anglican Settlement, were content to remain within the National Church in the hope of bringing about from within a further change in its polity and worship; only to be eventually forced into non-conformity by the Act of Uniformity in 1662. The Independents, however, were determined upon 'reformation without tarrying for any.'[2] Becoming convinced that conformity meant disobedience to the Word of God, they withdrew from the Anglican Church and set up conventicles of their own.[3] 'Whilst each party had a different method of church government, they were both united in accepting the same doctrine of the all-sufficiency of the Word of God in doctrinal and liturgical matters. Despite small differences in detail, they are substantially the same and their spiritual father is John Calvin.'[4]

[1] See Horton Davies, *The Worship of the English Puritans,* ch. ii.

[2] They are not, however, to be confused with the early Separatists. See ibid., ch. vii.

[3] See Strype, *Grindal* (Oxford, 1821), pp. 168f.

[4] Horton Davies, op. cit., p. 11.

Puritan worship, both Presbyterian and Independent, is therefore based upon the Reformed rite of Geneva. While the more extreme Separatists (Barrowists, Brownists and Anabaptists) repudiated all liturgical forms, including even the Lord's Prayer, the Puritans in general were not opposed to a liturgy as such. Their objection was to a particular liturgy, the Book of Common Prayer, on the grounds that it has 'too great affinity with the Form of the Church of Rome' and 'differeth too much from that which Churches elsewhere reformed allow and observe.'[1] Even so, the more conservative were prepared to accept the Prayer Book, at least provisionally, as long as its ceremonies were not enforced. John Knox's Genevan Service Book, however, was widely used and became 'the parent of Puritan worship both in Scotland and in England.'[2] It illustrates the essential characteristics of Puritan worship: 'The Word of God as the sufficient basis of Divine worship, and the apostolic simplicity as its precedent.' 'The phraseology of all prayers is Scriptural and it is equally significant that psalms are preferred to hymns since they are Scriptural. Similarly, the Lord's Prayer is used because of its Dominical authority. The centrality of the Sermon also testifies to the importance of the Word of God in worship.'[3] But the Puritans were opposed to any liturgical forms which excluded free or extemporary prayer, upon which the Independents in particular placed great emphasis.

The document most representative of seventeenth century Puritan worship is the Westminster Directory of 1644 which effects a compromise between order and freedom. It is essen-

[1] Hooker, *Eccl. Pol.,* V. xxvii. 1.

[2] Horton Davies, op. cit., p. 31.

[3] ibid., p. 32.

tially a Directory and not a Liturgy, giving general directions regarding the structure and content of worship and allowing for both liturgical and free prayer. Based upon the Scottish Book of Common Order, which is in turn derived from Knox's Genevan Service Book, it permits a wide variety of alternatives as a concession to the Independents. 'It is the first comprehensive attempt to find an order of worship which would prove acceptable to the whole body of Puritans, Presbyterian and Independent.'[1] And, as Davies points out, 'the very fact that it was possible for Independents and Presbyterians to arrive at an agreed syllabus for worship is sufficient indication that they held a common tradition in public worship and that there were not as many varieties of Puritan worship as there were conventicles.'[2]

Since the Puritans stood in the liturgical tradition of Geneva, their worship was eucharistic in structure. There is good evidence that the Communion of the Lord's Supper was celebrated weekly by the early English Independents,[3] although their later and more general practice has been a monthly celebration, as was the custom of the English Church in Geneva. This was also the custom of the English Baptists according to the *Broadmead Records*.[4] The English Presbyterians limited themselves to a quarterly Communion, influenced no doubt by the practice of their brethren in Scotland where celebrations were even more infrequent in country parishes. The sons of Geneva perpetuated Calvin's enforced practice and forgot his avowed aim. But the Puritans as a whole were true to their Genevan ancestry in that

[1] ibid., p. 141.

[2] ibid.

[3] ibid., pp. 206-7.

[4] *Broadmead Records* (Ed. Underhill, London, 1847), p. 57. The Baptists belong to the extreme left-wing of the Puritan movement.

the structure of their worship was largely the same both when the Lord's Supper was celebrated and when it was not. In the Westminster Directory, as Maxwell points out, 'the eucharistic office remained the norm of Sunday morning worship when there was no celebration.'[1] The central Sunday service of classic English Dissent—Presbyterian, Independent (or Congregational) and Baptist—is therefore a 'full' service of Ante-Communion 'setting out the whole story of what God has done for man both in creation and redemption';[2] it is not a Daily Office to which a sermon is added.

The Methodist Church does not share in the Puritan tradition. Its chief affinities are with eighteenth-century Anglicanism from which it sprang, although its glory lies in its own peculiar tradition stemming from the creative genius of John and Charles Wesley. In considering Methodist worship, it must be remembered that John Wesley was a high-churchman who always regarded the evangelistic and fellowship services which he organized among his followers as *supplementary* to the normal worship of the Anglican Church. 'Always behind the burning experience and Apostolic love of souls, which characterized this great man, there stands his institutional religion.[3] As J. E. Rattenbury points out, the first rule of the Methodist Bands was that each member 'be at Church and at the Lord's Table every week.'

When it is remembered that in 1744 weekly celebrations of Holy Communion were very rare in the Church of England, the insistence on this rule may seem surprising, but not to those

1 *Concerning Worship*, p. 28.

2 J. Marsh, op. cit., p. xii.

3 J. E. Rattenbury, *Vital Elements of Public Worship*, p. 77.

who know the balance of worship for which Wesley stood. In the background the Church with its services and objective worship were always in his mind.[1]

Both John and Charles Wesley never ceased to regard the Eucharist as the centre and norm of worship in which they found, as nowhere else, the meaning of the Cross.[2] In 1784 we find John Wesley giving the same counsel to the elders of the American Methodist Church as he gave to his Bands forty years earlier—the admonition to weekly Communion. And 'when he faced in America, and contemplated in England, separation from the ancient Church of his birth, he cared for nothing more than the preservation for his people of the old values.'[3]

V DECLINE, CONFUSION AND RENEWAL

The eighteenth century saw the beginning of a decline in the worship of all the British Protestant Churches. In the Church of England, as we have seen, Mattins came to replace both the Eucharist and Ante-Communion as the popular service of the Church—a fact which was to have a far-reaching influence on the worship of other communions. Among the Nonconformists—Presbyterians, Congregationalists and Baptists—the eucharistic norm of classic Puritan worship became obscured by an excessive emphasis upon preaching, and the stately liturgical prayers of the Reformed tradition were ousted by didactic extemporary utterances. After the death of John Wesley, Methodism too began to share in the general decline, losing the objective note and sacramental emphasis of its founders.

[1] ibid., p. 77.
[2] See J. E. Rattenbury, *The Eucharistic Hymns of John and Charles Wesley.*
[3] *Vital Elements of Public Worship*, p. 84.

The Oxford Movement in the middle of the last century marked the turning of the tide. The Tractarians aimed at restoring the Eucharist as the central act of worship in the Church of England and attempted to revive some of the ancient ceremonial which had formerly belonged to it. Unfortunately, however, 'at the hands of the second generation of Tractarians the movement in favour of ceremonial was carried to such lengths as to provoke loud outcries against what was vulgarly called 'Ritualism.'[1] The result has been the unhappy cleavage in the Church of England which persists to the present day.

In the Churches of the Puritan tradition also there have been, since the latter part of the nineteenth century, movements to improve and enrich worship. Unfortunately these have largely resulted in the assimilation of the structure of the central Sunday service to the structure of Anglican Morning Prayer. 'What was designed and intended for services of daily prayer, a beautiful but subsidiary order, has been adopted, with certain alterations, as the norm of the weekly worship in many of the non-Anglican Churches. This development, at a time when the standard of worship had declined, brought with it many new enrichments; but worship that takes its structure from Morning Prayer must inevitably lack the centrality and objectiveness which characterize the Eucharist or even Ante-Communion.'[2]

The reason, as Maxwell points out,[3] is that after nearly two hundred years of decadence the eucharistic norm of Reformed worship had been forgotten in the Presbyterian and Congregational Churches by all but a few scholars. In

[1] C. S. Phillips, op. cit., pp. 35-36.

[2] W. D. Maxwell, *An Outline of Christian Worship*, p. 167.

[3] See ibid., pp. 167-170.

the absence of the texts of the early Reformed services, the would-be liturgical reformers turned to the only available Protestant service book, the Book of Common Prayer. And, influenced by decadent Anglican practice, they took as their pattern what had become the popular parish worship of the Church of England, Morning Prayer. Hence 'in recent years many liturgical "reformers" have transformed the Calvinian norm by confusing it with Anglican Matins, and by bringing their Sunday morning worship into close conformity with it. A study of modern Reformed Service Books both in Europe and America will show how deeply embedded this confusion has become in present practice. It began only some forty years ago, and the date is marked for Scottish practice in *Euchologion* [a Book of Common Order issued by the Church Service Society], 1905, where it is stated :

It was resolved to change the order of public worship as follows : The Lord's Prayer to be said both by minister and congregation at the close of the first prayer, and the intercessions and thanksgiving to precede the sermon. From this resolution there were dissents, the chief reason besides the departure from Primitive and Reformed usage being that the Order of the Communion which is the normal service of the Church should be followed as closely as possible at other times.

Once resolved upon, the change spread rapidly and the error has persisted.'[1]

This phase of liturgical confusion is now, happily, passing. There are today abundant signs of a liturgical return, an increasing desire to deepen and enrich the worship of the Church. The Report of the Faith and Order Commission on 'Ways of Worship' (1951) calls attention to 'the extent to which a "liturgical movement" is to be found in Churches

[1] W. D. Maxwell, *Concerning Worship*, p. 29.

of widely differing traditions.'[1] In the Roman Catholic Church 'there certainly exists a very radical movement aiming at greater simplicity, plasticity and directness of liturgical forms; and drastic reformations may be expected before long from Rome.'[2] Continental Benedictine communities are endeavouring to recover the liturgical ideals of the Early Church and there is a growing desire for a more intelligent participation of the laity in the normal parish worship. The trend is towards a greater use of the vernacular and a simple sung Mass at which all present shall communicate. A similar movement is to be found in the Eastern Orthodox tradition. Nearly thirty years ago Friedrich Heiler wrote: 'The new thing that is stirring in the Eastern Church is that the laity are pressing for an active part in the liturgy. The congregation desires to be no longer a silent spectator of the sacred mystery-drama, but to share in celebrating the great mysteries.'[3]

In the Churches of the Reformation the same wind is blowing. The High Church Union and the Lutheran Liturgical Conference in Germany are attempting, from different points of view, to revivify the worship of the Lutheran Churches; a liturgical movement is gaining momentum in the Calvinistic Churches of Holland and Switzerland. As a result of the impetus given by the Oxford Movement, the Church of England is endeavouring to set its own house in order and restore the Parish Eucharist to its rightful place. Among Presbyterians C. F. Miller's protest that 'Our Scottish Kirk reformed is weekly offering a worship which derived from the Monasteries'[4] has not been unheeded, and

[1] p. 16.
[2] F. G. Van der Meer, 'Roman Catholic' in *Ways of Worship*, p. 45.
[3] *The Spirit of Worship*, p. 11.
[4] *Prayers for Parish Worship*, Introduction, p. xii.

discerning ministers are following W. D. Maxwell's lead in restoring the true norm of Reformed worship. Congregationalists now possess *A Book of Public Worship* 'confessedly compiled upon the recognition of the basic structure' of their Reformed rite and making available for all their churches some of the rich material to be found in their own liturgical traditions.[1] A Methodist, J. E. Rattenbury, appeals to modern Protestantism to 'restore, without losing subjective values, objectivity to its worship'[2] and recalls his own Church to John Wesley's ideal of a weekly celebration of Holy Communion.[3]

This modern liturgical movement, sacramental in its emphasis and ecumenical in its scope, is aptly summed up in a paragraph of the Faith and Order Commission's Report:

There is a widespread genuine unrest, a very definite feeling that worship ought to regain its central place in life, and that it can only do this if Churches return to the primitive patterns. To this end many Churches turn away from the habits and practices of their recent past in order to regain the purity and strength of worship as it was practised in their classic periods. Often it is not clear whether this return to the past constitutes any definite theologically justified movement. There is need to discriminate between the claims of tradition and the authority of Holy Scripture, between the felt attraction of what is old or 'classic,' and the need to base what is done on obedience to divine commandment. But in one way or another there is a desire to recover the 'original pattern.'[4]

1 See *A Book of Public Worship,* Introduction, p. xiii.

2 *Vital Elements of Public Worship,* p. 65.

3 ibid., p. 103.

4 *Ways of Worship,* p. 21.

CHAPTER III

The Ministry of the Word

'CHRISTIAN worship,' says W. H. Cadman, 'is at once the Word of God and the obedient response thereto.'[1] This not only epitomizes the fundamental theology of worship as response to revelation, man's *Antwort* to God's *Wort;* it also emphasizes the centrality of the Word in worship. The Word of God, from which it springs, is not external to the act of worship; it is of its very essence. This is the basic liturgical principle of the Reformation. The Roman Mass is essentially offering; the movement of the service is from man to God. But the movement of Reformed worship is from God to man; at its heart is the divine self-giving. That is precisely what the Reformers meant by the Word of God. Not just a word about God, or even a message from God. The Word is nothing less than the self-communication of God—God coming to us, meeting us in judgment and in mercy, imparting Himself to us in redeeming love; what Oscar Cullmann calls God in His revelatory action.[2] In short, by the Word we mean revelation, which P. T. Forsyth has defined as the self-bestowal of the living God: 'It is God Himself drawing ever more near and arriving at last.'[3]

Revelation is given in the stuff of history. In a series of crises in the history of their people, the prophets of Israel

[1] 'The Word of God in the New Testament' in *Christian Worship* (ed. N. Micklem), p. 67.

[2] *Christ and Time,* p. 24.

[3] *Positive Preaching and the Modern Mind,* p. 16.

discerned the mighty acts of the Lord through which He 'visited' His people in judgment and in mercy. Then, in the fulness of time, the Word became flesh in the Incarnation of the divine Son. First and foremost, therefore, Jesus Christ is God's Word. 'He Himself is the communication, the self-communication of God.'[1] As Forsyth puts it, 'It was by men that God gave Himself to men, till, in the fulness of time, He came for good and all in the God-man Christ, the living Word, in whom God was present, reconciling the world unto Himself.'[2]

God, who at sundry times and in divers manners spake in time past unto the fathers by the prophets, hath in these last days spoken unto us by His Son (Heb. i. 1-2).

And the Word was made flesh and dwelt among us . . . full of grace and truth (Jn. i. 14f).

There are three 'modes' by which this divine Word, uttered in God's mighty acts in history, declared by the prophets, incarnate in Jesus Christ, is conveyed to us—the Bible, Preaching, and the Sacraments. Of these, the Bible is primary.

1. *The Bible* is the record and interpretation of the events in time in which the Eternal God has visited and redeemed His people. It is the primary witness to these events and to God's saving activity manifested in and through them. The Old Testament tells of the calling and deliverance of the ancient People of God, their teaching through the prophets, the providential ordering of their national life, their training through the discipline of suffering. And running through it all is the deepening anticipation of the Kingdom and right-

[1] E. Brunner, *The Divine-Human Encounter*, p. 77.

[2] op. cit., p. 16.

eousness yet to be revealed. The prophetic insights and expectations of the Old Testament are fulfilled in the events which form the theme of apostles and evangelists in the New. In the fulness of time the Messiah is born, the Son of Man comes to seek and to save that which is lost, the Suffering Servant gives His life a ransom for many, the Heavenly King vanquishes death and the grave and opens the Kingdom of Heaven to all believers. And so the New Israel of God tastes the powers of the age to come as she adores her crucified and risen Lord, proclaims salvation through His name, and awaits His coming to judge the world.

The Bible is both the record and the instrument of this historical revelation: it is the medium of the Gospel of God's redeeming love in Jesus Christ. Through it the Wisdom of God and the Power of God are communicated to each generation of men. The written Word not only testifies to the Word made flesh; it mediates to us His presence and His saving love. Worship therefore, if it be dependent upon revelation, must have the Bible at its centre. It is through the reading of Holy Scripture from pulpit or lectern that the assembled Church is confronted anew with the biblical revelation, in response to which alone it can offer worship in Spirit and in truth. The Bible has thus a unique place in Christian worship. It cannot be replaced by any other literature, however venerable and 'inspired.' Homer and Virgil, Shakespeare and Milton, Tennyson and Keats may confront us with the eternal values of beauty, truth and goodness; but they do not set forth the great saving acts of God by which He has revealed Himself to man. They do not mediate to us the unique self-bestowal of the living God in the life and history of Israel, culminating in a cradle, a cross, and an empty tomb.

Furthermore, since worship is the Church's obedient response to the saving acts of God, these saving acts must be set forth before the response can be evoked: the *Wort* must precede the *Antwort*. It follows that the Bible, in which's God's redemptive action is declared, must be read *early* in the service if the praise, prayer and offering of the congregation are to be a true response to the divine Word. Failure to grasp this simple principle results in liturgical chaos. The writer has on his files a collection of Orders of Service gathered in both hemispheres. While some are excellent, others are little more than a string of 'items,' the arrangement of which displays neither liturgical nor any other kind of logic. And the most common defect is that there is no reading of Holy Scriptures until relatively late in the service. The proper order of *Wort* and *Antwort* is thus reversed. When Thanksgiving, Intercession and Offering precede the reading and hearing of the Word of God to which they are essentially the response, the theological basis of worship is destroyed. Worship ceases to be dependent upon revelation. Lacking theological direction and constraint, it becomes at the mercy of ministerial vagaries; there is nothing to ensure or guarantee its specifically Christian character.

Worship properly begins with an Approach in praise and penitence. This leads directly to the central part of the service—the Ministry of the Word in which the Scriptures of the Old and New Testaments are read and heard, and some portion of them is expounded. There should normally be Lessons from *both* the Old and the New Testaments. The biblical revelation is a unity: Old and New Testaments are complementary parts of one organic whole. The Old Testament cannot be understood apart from the events which constitute the theme of the New; the New Testament is not to be isolated from the background and preparation which the Old provides. *Novum Testamentum in Vetere latet; Vetus Testamentum in Novo patet*—the New is in the Old concealed; the Old is in the New revealed. Hence each interprets and elucidates the other. The Bible, with all its rich diversity, tells one story—the story of our salvation.

> It begins with the tale of a garden,
> And ends with the city of gold.

It is the story of a covenant relationship between God and man. But this story is in two parts: volume one tells of the Old Covenant made with Abraham and ratified with his descendants, the ancient People of God; volume two declares the New Covenant in the blood of Christ made with the New Israel, the Christian Church. Readings from both parts of the story are necessary, therefore, if anything of its wholeness is to be set forth.

In the worship of the early Church there were numerous Scripture lections from both Testaments, but by the end of the fourth century they became reduced to three—one from the Old Testament and two from the New. One of the latter was selected from the apostolic Epistles (or Acts or Revelation) and the other from a Gospel. During the fifth century the 'prophetic lection,' as the Old Testament reading was called, disappeared from the West leaving only the Epistle and Gospel in the Mass.[1] This omission is perpetuated in the Book of Common Prayer: the Anglican Communion Office has no Old Testament lection. It is possible, as Archdeacon Harrison points out, to regard the Ten Commandments as a fixed Old Testament Lesson. He

[1] The 'prophetic lection,' along with other ancient characteristics of the Mass, is retained during Holy Week.

rightly adds, however, that 'the re-introduction of a prophetic lection, before the Epistle, would have everything to recommend it.'[1]

In a full diet of worship all three Scripture Lessons are necessary for an adequate setting forth of the biblical revelation in the Christian perspective.[2] The Old Testament reading, which should generally (although not necessarily) be taken from one of the prophetic books, tells of the preparation for the coming of Christ in the life and history of Israel; the Epistle testifies to the fellowship 'in Christ' of the New Israel; while in the Gospel the words and deeds of our Lord Himself are set forth. 'Thus only can Holy Scripture be read in its Christian proportion and balance.'[3] The Lessons should be read in this order, the Gospel having the place of honour at the end as the seal of the Scriptures. The practice of the congregation standing for the reading of the Gospel Lesson goes back at least to the third century and is a fitting expression of reverence.[4]

From early times the Scripture lections have been interspersed with the singing of psalms. When in the West the

[1] op. cit., p. 77.

[2] The structure of the chief Sunday service should be eucharistic, whether there be a celebration of Holy Communion or not. See chapter IV. In the other service, where an 'office' structure is appropriate, it is not necessary to have the three lections. There should normally, however, be a Lesson both from the Old and from the New Testament.

[3] W. D. Maxwell, *Concerning Worship*, p. 32.

[4] See the so-called Canons of Addai (3rd century), Cureton's *Ancient Syriac Documents,* p. 27: 'At the conclusion of all the Scriptures let the Gospel be read, as the seal of all the Scriptures; and let the people listen to it standing up on their feet, because it is the glad tidings of the salvation of all men.'

lections became reduced to Epistle and Gospel, there remained only the intervening 'Gradual' psalm, so called because it was originally sung from the *gradus*—the step either of the sanctuary or of the reader's desk (*ambo*). Duchesne points out that this ancient chanting of psalms between the Scripture Lessons was a formal re-presentation of the Psalter, not to be confused with the other chants of the Mass—the Introit, Offertory and Communion—which were added later to sustain devotion by 'filling in' during long ceremonies. 'The gradual and similar chants had an intrinsic value, and during the time in which they were sung there was nothing else going on.'[1]

When the three lections are restored, it is now customary to read them in two groups between which a 'gradual' psalm in prose or metre should be sung.[2] Either the Old Testament Lesson may stand alone, the two New Testament Lessons—Epistle and Gospel—being read together after the psalm; or the Epistle may follow the Old Testament lection, then the psalm, and finally the Gospel. The former grouping, preserving the clear distinction between the Old and New Testaments, is the more general. The latter, however, has the merit of giving greater prominence to the Gospel reading. In some places the responsive reading of a psalm has replaced the chant. This is permissible (though not desirable) in services having an 'office' structure. The psalms, however, are meant to be sung, and the 'gradual' psalm in a service of eucharistic structure should always be sung, preferably as a prose chant, but otherwise in a

[1] L. Duchesne, *Christian Worship: Its Origin and Evolution*, p. 169.

[2] This assumes that the structure of the service is eucharistic. In the 'office' structure the psalms *precede* the Scripture lections between which a canticle or hymn is sung. See chapter V.

metrical version. Because they are essentially acts of praise, the psalms (with some exceptions) are not suitable for reading as a lection. A psalm read responsively by minister and people must not be confused with the Old Testament Lesson, therefore. The latter is the prophetic Word; the former, an act of praise.

The Scripture Lessons are most appropriately introduced and concluded by one or other of the classic formulæ. The Prayer Book offices of Morning and Evening Prayer contain the rubric:

Note that before every Lesson the Minister shall say, Here beginneth such a Chapter, *or* Verse of such a Chapter, of such a Book: *And after every Lesson,* Here endeth the First, *or* the Second Lesson.

In the Order for Holy Communion the rubric is:

And immediately after the Collect the Priest shall read the Epistle, saying, The Epistle (*or,* The portion of Scripture appointed for the Epistle) is written in the — Chapter of — beginning at the — Verse. *And the Epistle ended, he shall say,* Here endeth the Epistle. *Then shall he read the Gospel* (*the people all standing up*) *saying,* The holy Gospel is written in the — Chapter of — beginning at the — Verse.

In the Reformed tradition, however, the classic introduction is:

Let us hear the Word of God (or, Hear the Word of God), as it is contained (or, written) in the Book of —, the — chapter, at the — verse.

This emphasizes the true nature of what follows—the reading and hearing of the Word of God. Both the First and the Second Lessons are introduced in this way. After the First, it is sufficient to say:

Here endeth the First (or, the Old Testament) Lesson,

Or after each of the lections there may be said respectively:

Here endeth the reading from the Old Testament;
Here endeth the Epistle;
Thanks be to Thee, O Lord, for this thy glorious Gospel.

At the conclusion of the Scripture lections the reader says:

The Lord bless to us the reading of His holy Word, and to His name be glory and praise.[1]

The reading of Holy Scripture, although in practice divided into two or three lections, is nevertheless *one* primary act in Christian worship. It is the setting forth of the divine revelation, the declaration of the mighty acts of God for us men and for our salvation, to which everything else is the response. For this reason the different readings should be kept together, separated only by a psalm, canticle or hymn. They should not be dispersed to different parts of the service, as is sometimes erroneously done; neither should they be separated by any major act of worship. The biblical revelation is a unity and Christian worship is the response to this revelation *as a whole*.

The purpose of a creed, or a confession of faith, in worship is to set forth the whole Gospel of which the Scripture lections have proclaimed a part. It epitomizes the Christian revelation to which the Bible as a whole bears witness. The recital by the congregation of a creed or a confession of faith is therefore a fitting conclusion to the readings from the Old and New Testaments: the parts are seen in the light of the whole.

There is no valid reason why Free Churchmen should

[1] 'At the conclusion of holy Scripture, a most objectionable formula is sometimes heard: "The Lord *add* His blessing to the reading of the Word." As Dr. John White has said, "The blessing is in the Word; why therefore pray for it as an addition?"' W. D. Maxwell, *Concerning Worship*, p. 56.

not use the great creeds of the Church in their worship. There is only one Christian Faith—the Faith proclaimed by the apostolic preaching to which the New Testament bears witness; and it is this Faith which is expressed in the historic creeds. It is the faith of the whole Church—the Catholic Faith. The modern sectarian association of the word 'Catholic' is one of the ironies of history. Derived as it is from the Greek *katholikos,* meaning 'universal' or 'whole,' it is not the monopoly of that branch of the Christian Church which owns allegiance to the Bishop of Rome. And the 'mission from Rome' has no claim to its exclusive use. Just as the same joy and peace in believing is shared by Francis of Assisi and John Wesley, Thomas Aquinas and John Knox, Martin Luther and St. Paul, so also the same essential truths of the Faith are held by Roman Catholic and Methodist, Anglican and Presbyterian, Lutheran and Baptist, Greek Orthodox and Congregationalist. Far-reaching differences, both theological and ecclesiological, there are indeed; and they may not be minimized. But fundamentally it is the same historic Faith that they all share.

The Catholic Faith is summarized in what is known as the Apostles' Creed. This is in essence the ancient Baptismal Creed of the Church of Rome which can be traced back to the second century, though it did not reach its present form till the seventh or eighth century. This creed and the so-called Nicene Creed which emphasizes the absolute divinity of our Lord—'God of God, Light of Light, Very God of Very God. . . . Being of one substance with the Father'—are statements of the Church's Faith which were drawn up in the first four centuries before any of the present divisions arose. And they are accepted substantially, even if not used, by all the orthodox branches of the Church today. Admittedly some of the Puritans objected to them, but it was on the grounds of their association with Roman Catholic usage; they had no quarrel with their content.[1] This is clearly stated in John Owen's classic defence of the seventeenth-century dissenters:

They are such as believe and make open profession of all the articles of the Christian faith; they do so as they are declared in the Scripture; nor is the contrary charged on them. There is nothing determined by the ancient councils to belong unto Christian faith which they disbelieve; nor do they own any doctrine condemned by them. . . . They own the doctrine of the Church of England as established by law, in nothing receding from it; nor have they any novel or uncatholic opinion of their own.[2]

Congregationalists, it is true, have always refused to impose any creed as a test of the Christian Faith or to make acceptance of any formula a condition of church membership. But they have never repudiated the classic creeds of the Church; they have merely refused to be bound to express their faith in any prescribed form of words, and especially in forms that were used by the Roman Church. The seventeenth-century Independents, as Congregationalists were then called, did however produce their own confession of faith—the *Savoy Declaration* of 1658, which is entirely in line with the historic creeds.

The historic English Free Churches are not sects; they stand in the central dogmatic tradition of Christendom. The great ecumenical creeds are part of their heritage. They could well enrich their worship.

To return to the Bible: through the reading of the Old and New Testaments there is re-presented in each service of

[1] See Horton Davies, op. cit., Appendix C, pp. 273f.

[2] *A Letter Concerning the Matter of the Present Excommunications.*

worship some great theme of the Christian story, the whole of which is epitomized in the creed. If there is to be an adequate presentation of the biblical revelation, the Scripture Lessons must be planned so that central passages of the Bible are read week by week and during the course of a year all the great themes of the Christian story are set forth.[1] This is best done by using a lectionary which follows the Christian Year. As Father Hebert observes, 'A fixed lectionary, if well arranged, covers the whole ground, and saves the congregation from the frequent repetition of the minister's favourite texts. But there are occasions when a free choice is indispensable.'[2]

The Christian Year, it must be emphasized, is an essential part of liturgical structure. Worship consists of both *Wort* and *Antwort*—God's Word and man's response thereto. 'The Gospel must be announced if men are truly to give glory to God.[3] Hence, as Archdeacon Harrison points out, 'the essential principle of liturgy is not the use of set forms but the setting forth of the saving acts of God, and, above all else, of the Cross of Christ.'[4] The minister, however, cannot present the whole Gospel each Sunday. But he must present the whole Gospel; and the Christian Year, as an extension of this fundamental liturgical principle, provides the framework.

That year is built round the cardinal points of the life of our Lord; Christmas commemorates His birth, Epiphany His baptism and universal mission, Passiontide and Easter His death

[1] Cf. *The Book of Common Order* of the United Church of Canada, p. v: 'The Lord's people should hear the great passages of Scripture at least once a year.'

[2] A. G. Hebert, 'Anglican' in *Ways of Worship*, p. 75.

[3] D. E. W. Harrison, *The Book of Common Prayer*, p. 11.

[4] ibid., p. 15.

and resurrection, Whitsuntide the gift of His Spirit. It is thus that, one by one, the acts of God in Christ for men become in turn the special emphasis of the Church's worship; yet always they are set within the framework of His whole life and the perfection of His saving work.[1]

In the liturgical tradition of the West provision is made for the observance of the Christian Year by a variable part of the liturgy known as 'The Proper.' This consists of the special lessons, psalms and prayers appointed for each season. The creed as used in worship places what is particular to a given Sunday in the context of the whole Faith.

Free Church ministers, who are responsible for the preparation of suitable prayers as well as the selection of appropriate lessons, psalms and hymns,[2] will find valuable help in the Church of Scotland *Prayers for the Christian Year* and *Prayers and Services for Christian Festivals* compiled for the use of Congregationalists by the Reverend J. M. Todd. Lectionaries providing lessons for each Sunday of the Christian Year, and also for special occasions, are contained in the *Book of Common Order* of the Church of Scotland and the Congregational *Book of Public Worship*.[3]

But what version of the Bible should be read in Church? —the Authorized Version of 1611? or the Revised Version of 1885? or a modern translation? The Revised Version is certainly a more accurate translation, but it lacks the

[1] ibid., p. 15. Cf. C. F. Miller, *Prayers for Parish Worship*, Introduction, p. xiii: 'The Christian Year is a presentation in liturgical symbols of the Christian view of history as the acting out of the drama of God's redemption of the world. It is all history, past, present, and to come, which is acted out on the stage of the liturgical year.'

[2] See pp. 131ff. for the liturgical use of hymns in Free Church worship.

[3] See also the *St. Andrew's Lectionary*.

rhythm and literary beauty of the Authorized Version; and its marginal readings frequently give a better rendering of the original than does the text. Of modern translations that Dr. James Moffatt is the most widely known and perhaps the best; but considered as a whole it is more suitable for private reading than for public use. The recent American Revised Standard Version, however, is an excellent translation into modern English which preserves something at least of the dignity and rhythm of the Authorized Version. But even this lacks the literary beauty, to say nothing of the devotional associations, of the Authorized Version. The latter are more important than is often realized and are frequently overlooked when this question is discussed. The Authorized Version rendering of Isa. liii, for example, has for the mature Christian rich overtones which are missing from the most flawless translation into modern idiom.

As a general rule, therefore, the Authorized Version is to be preferred for the normal services of worship. When, however, its translation is clearly defective, or its text obscure, either the Revised Version or the Revised Standard Version may well be substituted. There is also a place for the occasional use of a modern translation, like that of Moffatt or J. B. Phillips, which clarifies the meaning of a passage by a free paraphrase. This applies particularly to passages whose significance has become blunted by familiarity. Moffatt's rendering of 1 Cor. xiii, for example, frequently 'comes home' to the hearer and stabs the conscience broad awake far more effectively than does the Authorized Version:

Love is very patient, very kind. Love knows no jealousy; love makes no parade, gives itself no airs, is never rude, never selfish, never irritated, never resentful; love is never glad when others go wrong, love is gladdened by goodness, always slow to expose, always eager to believe the best, always hopeful, always patient.

Similarly, J. B. Phillips, in his translation of a passage like 2 Cor. iv. 7f, makes St. Paul's words live:

This priceless treasure we hold, so to speak, in a common earthenware jar—to show that the splendid power of it belongs to God and not to us. We are handicapped on all sides, but we are never frustrated; we are puzzled, but never in despair. We are persecuted, but we never have to stand it alone: we may be knocked down but we are never knocked out! Every day we experience something of the death of the Lord Jesus, so that we may also know the power of the life of Jesus in these bodies of ours. We are always facing death, but this means that you know more and more of life.

For youth services and on the radio there is much to be said for the judicious use of modern translations such as these. In the normal worship of the Church, however, they should be used sparingly and only when there is some good reason for departing from the Authorized Version.

The Bible has another liturgical function quite distinct from its formal reading in Church. Not only does it declare the divine revelation, the Word of God to which worship is the Church's response; it also provides the liturgical form[1] and devotional language of that response. Alan Richardson reminds us that 'there is, in fact, a biblical language which always has been and always must be the language of the Church. . . . The Bible has its own language, and even if many of the words which it uses are words which one might encounter any day in a secular newspaper, they always keep their own biblical meaning, which is usually not the same as

[1] See chapter IV, pp. 96ff.

the newspaper meaning. One thinks, for instance, of such words as "love," "freedom," "life," "death," "hope " and so on.' There are other more distinctively biblical words such as 'righteousness,' 'sin,' 'judgement,' 'forgiveness,' 'salvation,' 'thanksgiving,' 'repentance,' 'faith,' 'chastisement,' besides biblical words whose meaning has been secularized—'peace,' 'service,' 'fellowship,' 'justice.' The biblical language is not peculiar to any one version, or indeed tongue, since 'the distinctively biblical meaning of the words shines through all the various translations.'[1]

This distinctively biblical language always has been and always must be the language of worship. 'Our study has made clear,' says the Faith and Order Commission on Ways of Worship, 'that the traditional forms of liturgy are throughout scriptural, both in their spirit and in their choice of language.'[2] Similarly, in the traditional forms of 'Free' worship, 'this freedom is rigorously controlled by the knowledge of Scripture, the words and thoughts of which are the field in which freedom to move is given.' And for this reason, 'there is often in each tradition a common underlying structure.'[3]

Free Church ministers should ponder this fact. No worship can be in spirit and in truth unless it is thoroughly biblical in its inspiration and content. The Sermon should indeed 'contemporize' the Gospel by interpreting the biblical language and conveying its meaning—as far as this can be done—in thought-forms and words which are familiar to the hearers, always being sure that it is the *biblical* truth

[1] See *Preface to Bible-Study,* pp. 84f.

[2] *Ways of Worship,* p. 18.

[3] ibid., p. 19.

that is conveyed.[1] In public prayer, however, the local congregation is joining in *corporate* worship—the worship of the whole Body of Christ, militant on earth and triumphant in heaven. Here colloquialisms and provincialisms are out of place and a secular vocabulary is quite inadequate for the adoration of the Creator who is also the Redeemer of mankind and for the expression of man's deepest needs. The divine language is the tongue of the divine Society. It links the worship of the Church militant on earth with that of the Church triumphant in heaven.

Most of us are like refugees, when we first enter the gates of our adopted country; we speak the language of the New Jerusalem badly and with a foreign accent. The Bible is our book of words, from which we learn to converse fluently with the old inhabitants—apostles, saints and martyrs, a great company which cannot be numbered, gathered in from many kindreds and lands and tongues. Within the walls of the city the language of the Church is spoken, and God is worshipped in the words of the Psalmists and hymn-writers and liturgy-makers who are masters of the divine vocabulary, and every man speaks in this new tongue, as the Spirit gives him utterance.[2]

2. *Preaching* is the second 'mode' of the Word in worship. 'The Church's preaching is the Word of God in a derivative and tertiary sense. It is derived from the secondary sense, the Bible, which, in its turn, is derived from the primary sense, Jesus Christ.[3] P. T. Forsyth begins his search-

1 'The demand for a "non-theological language" very often hides a dislike, not of words, but of the theological truths which lie behind them. . . . Too often the attempt to avoid "theological" language and to use only an ordinary workaday vocabulary has resulted in the substitution of a prudential ethical or topical address in the place of real Christian preaching.' Alan Richardson, op. cit., p. 84.

2 ibid., pp. 92-93.

3 R. H. Fuller, *Theology*, vol. xlvii, p. 271.

ing and stimulating book, *Positive Preaching and the Modern Mind,* by the bold assertion that with its preaching Christianity stands or falls. But what precisely is preaching? And why does it occupy such a prominent place in Reformed worship? The late Dr. Campbell Morgan defined it as 'the declaration of the grace of God to human need on the authority of the Throne of God; and it demands on the part of those who hear that they show obedience to the thing declared.'[1]

The two Greek words most generally used of preaching in the New Testament are *euangelizomai,* 'to announce good news.' and *kērussō,* 'to proclaim as a herald (*kērux*). Both indicate the essential nature of preaching as proclamation. It is not to be confused with oratory. A sermon is something quite different from a lecture or an address. 'The pulpit is another place, and another kind of place, from the platform. . . . The Christian preacher is not the successor of the Greek orator, but of the Hebrew prophet. The orator comes with but an inspiration, the prophet comes with a revelation.'[2] The object of a lecture is to convey truth. The lecturer is a teacher whose aim is to inform and illuminate the mind. Hence 'not every lecture is designed to alter its auditors, but preaching proposes to make men different.[3] An address presents a point of view and attempts to stimulate the interest of the hearers in some particular subject. It may have as its end the promotion of specific action on behalf of some particular cause. But 'it is one thing to have to rouse or persuade people to do something, to put themselves into something; it is another to

[1] *Preaching,* p. 15.

[2] P. T. Forsyth, op. cit., p. 3.

[3] H. S. Coffin, *What to Preach,* p. 155.

have to induce them to trust somebody and renounce themselves for him.'[1]

The preaching of the Gospel is concerned with news, not views; it is the proclamation of Good News, not the tendering of good advice. For this reason it has that sense of urgency which characterizes the herald. J. S. Whale has expressed this in a telling passage which merits quoting at length:[2]

You remember how they brought the good news from Ghent to Aix and what a truly dramatic lyric Browning makes of it. Three men, galloping into the midnight, with news that was to save a city. Speed was everything. In silence they kept the great pace. At dawn one horse staggers and dies with a groan, and only two are left. When the spire of Aix begins to show white in the distance and Joris gasps, 'How they'll greet us!' —his horse suddenly rolls over, dead as a stone; and all hangs now on a solitary horseman.

> Then I cast loose my buffcoat, each holster let fall,
> Shook off both my jack-boots, let go belt and all,
> Clapped my hands, laughed and sang, any noise—bad or
> good,
> Till at length into Aix Rolland galloped and stood.
> And all I remember is friends flocking round. . .

News-telling is there summed up, not only for the seventeenth but for every century. . . . The man has a message. It does not depend on him for its credibility or authority, as it would do if he were galloping to tell the world his private fancies and latest excogitations. The message has the objectivity of what is given by the stuff of events. It has the concreteness which belongs not to what might happen and might be true but to what has verily happened and is amazingly gloriously true. He has

[1] P. T. Forsyth, op. cit., p. 4.

[2] *What is a Living Church?* pp. 60-61.

made it his own, yet it is not his message but the message of the one who sent him. This man delivers what he has received.

Urgency is not the distinctive quality of preaching however. It is essentially a sacramental act through which the redemptive action of God in Christ is mediated. 'In true preaching, as in a true sacrament, more is done than said.'[1] The classic Protestant conception of preaching is comparable to the Catholic view of the Mass.[2] Both are concerned with the mediation of the Real Presence of Christ: each is dependent upon the spoken word—for one, the word of the preacher; for the other, the word of the priest: in the case of either the result is nothing less than a miracle. The Roman Catholic believes that when the priest recites the Words of Institution: *Hoc est enim corpus meum*—'This is my body . . .', a miracle happens—the substance of the bread and wine is changed into the substance of the body and blood of Christ; Christ Himself is present on the altar. The Protestant holds that when the preacher proclaims the Gospel of a Crucified and Risen Lord, something equally miraculous takes place—Christ manifests Himself in judgment and in mercy to those who hear; He Himself is present challenging men to repentance, decision and faith. *Praedicatio Verbi Dei est Verbum Dei* said Luther—'The preaching of the Word of God *is* the Word of God.' He meant that when the mighty acts of God in Christ for us men and for our salvation are faithfully declared, He Himself

[1] P. T. Forsyth, op. cit., p. 81. Cf. ibid., p. 80: 'The preacher's place in the Church is sacramental. . . . He mediates the word to the Church from faith to faith, from his faith to theirs, from one stage of their common faith to another. . . . He is a living element in Christ's hands (broken, if need be) for the distribution and increment of Grace.'

[2] This does not imply that preaching can in any way take the place of the sacrament of Holy Communion.

speaks to the hearts and consciences of men. And not only speaks but *acts*. 'No true preaching of the Cross can be other than part of the action of the Cross. . . . The real presence of Christ crucified is what makes preaching. It is what makes of a speech a sermon, and of a sermon Gospel. This is the work of God, this continues His work in Christ.'[1] The effectiveness of a sermon does not depend upon the eloquence of the preacher, or the cogency of his logic, or the clarity of his thought; it depends upon the power of God. No mere words of the minister can of themselves lead men to repentance and faith; that is the work of Christ 'in, with and under' the minister's words. It is not by human speech, however moving, that Christians are renewed in the spirit of their minds; it is by the operation of the Holy Ghost.

The mystery of preaching is therefore that through it the everlasting Gospel is contemporized, and not only contemporized but individualized, and not merely individualized but actualized. The proclamation that God so loved the world that He gave His only begotten Son, that whosoever believeth in Him should not perish but have everlasting life, comes home with the compelling conviction that He loved *me* and gave Himself for *me*. And I am apprehended by the Crucified and Risen Lord as really as was St. Paul on the Damascus road, so that I am constrained to say, 'Lord, what wilt Thou have me to do?' This is not the work of man; it is the work of God.

Preaching is that divine, saving activity in history, which began two thousand years ago in the advent of Christ and in His personal relationships with men and women, and has continued throughout the ages in the sphere of redeemed personal relationships (which is the true Church), now focusing on me,

[1] P. T. Forsyth, op. cit., p. 82.

confronting me, as a person indissolubly bound up with other persons at this present time. . . . It is not merely *telling* me something. It is God actively probing me, challenging my will, calling on me for decision, offering me His succour, through the only medium which the nature of His purpose permits Him to use, the medium of a personal relationship.[1]

Such preaching is prophetic: through it rings the inescapable note, 'Thus saith the Lord.' Without this there may be eloquence and learning and popular appeal; but there can be no true preaching. It is precisely this prophetic note that is so often lacking in the modern pulpit, and the parlous condition of many churches gives point to Forsyth's warning that with its preaching Christianity stands or falls. As J. E. Rattenbury observes, 'Nothing has the immediate power of bringing to mankind the glory and grace of God, that can be compared with the words of a man who is plainly a messenger, an ambassador of Heaven, saying with authority "Be ye reconciled to God".' And he rightly warns us that any type of service, or ministerial training, or academic standards, which suppresses this man, repeats the most fatal errors of Rome.[2] Preaching is not an optional extra for those who like it; it is a vital element in the Church's life. The Reformers were right when they insisted that the faithful preaching and hearing of the Word of God, as well as the administration of the Gospel Sacraments according to the ordinance of Christ, is an essential mark of the true Church. 'Through the preacher, the creative work of God in Christ goes on. Through his agency, there is continued "all that Jesus began both to do and teach." The Christian preacher is an instrument by which the Church, the Body of Christ,

[1] H. H. Farmer, *The Servant of the Word,* pp. 27-28.

[2] *Vital Elements of Public Worship,* pp. 96-97.

fulfils its function as "the extension of the Incarnation".'[1]

Since preaching is essentially the proclamation of the Gospel, the declaration of God's mighty acts in sacred history, it must be biblical to be true to type. The time-honoured custom of preaching from a text is no mere ecclesiastical convention. It signifies that the sermon springs from the written Word, it has its roots in the Bible. Hence it is, as Forsyth maintains, 'the outward sign of the objectivity of our religion, its positivity, its quality as something given to our hand.'[2] A sermon is not necessarily biblical, however, because it is prefaced by a Scripture text. This may be only a peg on which the preacher hangs his thoughts, or an opening quotation—the spring-board from which he plunges into his discourse. Again, biblical preaching is not preaching *about* the Bible; it is the exposition of Holy Scripture itself as the living and abiding Word of God.

This may take different forms, of course, and the wise preacher will vary his approach and his emphasis. A sermon may be topical and still biblical. The acid test is: Does it proclaim the Word? Does it declare the Gospel? Does it lift up Christ?

Sermons may be classified in several different ways. There is the two-fold classification made familiar by C. H. Dodd:[3] Kerugma and Didache—the 'preaching' sermon and the 'teaching' sermon. The difference is a difference of emphasis: the 'preaching' sermon, being essentially the proclamation of Christ crucified for our sins and raised for our justification, must convey some teaching of the significance of these historic facts; and the 'teaching' sermon is

[1] F. D. Coggan, *The Ministry of the Word,* p. 18.

[2] op. cit., p. 8.

[3] See *The Apostolic Preaching and its Developments.*

concerned with the exposition of some aspect of the Gospel of salvation through Christ or it is not a sermon at all.

Then there is the six-fold classification of sermons as Expository, Doctrinal, Ethical, Apologetic, Topical and Evangelistic. Here again there is no water-tight distinction and the same Gospel is common to them all. The expository sermon is a systematic exposition of some portion of the Bible—it may be a whole Book, or part of a Book, of the Old or New Testament; or perhaps a prophecy, or a parable, or some other part of the teaching of our Lord or of one of the apostles. The doctrinal sermon expounds some aspect of Christian doctrine—the Creation, the Incarnation, the Atonement, the Holy Trinity, the Church, the Last Things. The implications of the Gospel for Christian conduct in some particular sphere form the theme of the ethical sermon. It may be concerned with the common virtues of, for example, honesty, truthfulness, courtesy, perseverance; or with home-life, sex and marriage; or with some social issue like gambling, temperance, industrial relationships, war. In the apologetic sermon the approach is philosophical: the preacher, as 'defender of the Faith,' sets forth one or other of the grounds on which Christians may give a reason for the hope that is within them. The topical sermon attempts to evaluate some contemporary situation or current event, or a popular book, play or film in the light of the Christian Faith. Used sparingly, it has an important place, particularly in the pulpit of a city church. The danger is that it may easily degenerate into nothing more than a humanistic analysis of the topic and the preacher's reflections thereon. Such preaching, so-called, has lost its distinctively Christian character; hence it no longer possesses any 'sacramental' power. As Forsyth observes, 'The public soon grow weary of topical preaching alone, or newspaper preaching, in which the week's events supply the text and the Bible only an opening quotation.'[1] Finally, the aim of the evangelistic sermon is to lead the hearers to a definite act of committal to Christ.

A further classification is required for three particular types of sermon—the biographical sketch, the exposition of a biblical incident, and the sermon built around some unifying motif. Alexander Whyte's *Bible Characters* are superb illustrations of the first: the Gospel is expounded in terms of the triumphs and failures of men and women like Gideon and Michal, Eunice and St. Paul. The second type consists of the running exposition of a particular incident such as Jacob's wrestling at Jabbok or Jesus' walking on the sea. The third makes use of what has come to be known as the project method. The unifying motif may be, for instance, the mountains of the Bible—Sinai, the mount of law; Hermon, the mount of vision; Calvary, the mount of sacrifice; Olivet, the mount of promise.

Whatever be the form and emphasis of preaching, the sermon, if it is to be truly biblical, must be Christo-centric. If the preacher begins in the Old Testament, he must end in the New; if he starts from an Epistle, he must finish with the Gospel. The purpose of the written Word is to lead to the Word made flesh. The Scriptures testify to the Son. As Luther used to say, they are the swaddling clothes around the Babe, the crib in which Christ is laid. Christ is the centre of the Bible: the Old Testament leads up to Him; the New Testament declares Him. And He is the centre, not only chronologically, but in the sense that He is its unifying principle: in Him the whole biblical revelation

[1] op. cit., p. 9.

comes to a burning focus. Scripture can only be rightly interpreted, therefore, in the light of its 'fulfilment' in Christ: the part must be related to the whole. Hence 'biblical preaching preaches the Gospel and uses the Bible, it does not preach the Bible and use the Gospel.[1] The preacher's pattern is Philip expounding Isa. liii. to the Ethiopian eunuch: beginning at the same scripture, he preaches unto him Jesus.[2]

To preach Christ is to proclaim salvation through His Name. Christ is not truly preached when He is merely presented as the great Teacher of mankind, or extolled as the supreme Example of disinterested love. This was not the message of the men who turned the world upside down. 'The driving-force of the early Christian mission was not propaganda of beautiful ideals of the brotherhood of man; it was proclamation of the mighty acts of God.' The Christian religion is 'not a summary of the ways men ought to act in an ideal society, but an account of the way in which God has acted in history decisively and for ever.'[3] Jesus was not just a great prophet like Isaiah proclaiming the ways of God to men, or a great teacher like Socrates apprehending and unveiling eternal truth, or a great martyr like Joan of Arc giving His life for some high and noble cause. He was God manifest in the flesh for us men and for our salvation. He came, not just to point to the way, or to teach the truth, or to exemplify the life; He *is* the way, the truth, and the life. Salvation is not through His teaching but through His Person and Work. The heart of the Gospel, as T. W. Manson has said, is not the Sermon on the Mount

[1] P. T. Forsyth, op. cit., p. 37.

[2] See Acts viii. 35.

[3] J. S. Stewart, *Heralds of God,* pp. 63-66.

but the Cross on the Hill.[1] Hence 'to preach Christ really means to preach the Cross where His person took effect as the incarnation and the agent of the atoning grace of God.'[2] Here is the scandal of the Gospel: Christ crucified is still a stumbling-block to the Jews and foolishness to the Greeks: only to those who believe is He the power of God and the wisdom of God. To preach Christ, therefore, is to call men and women to faith in Him. And faith means what the Germans call *Entscheidung*—decision. The preacher must confront men with the inescapable question: What think ye of Christ? 'That is not preaching which is not preaching for a verdict.'[3]

Such preaching requires the most thorough and searching preparation of heart and mind—a preparation that is not confined to the making of particular sermons week by week but which exercises the whole personality of the preacher during the whole of his life. Sermon preparation is of two kinds—direct and indirect, the latter being by far the more important. Direct preparation goes on in the minister's study when he consults the commentaries and lexicons on next Sunday morning's text. But the real quality of his sermon will depend upon a disciplined spirit and a well-stored mind, a deep knowledge of the people to whom he speaks and a vital experience of the saving power of God. All that contributes to these things is the preacher's indirect preparation for his work, and its importance cannot be over-estimated. Where it is lacking, preaching may have brilliance but it will lack depth. The sermon which relies only upon the books consulted in the previous week will be

[1] *The Mission and Message of Jesus,* p. 301.

[2] P. T. Forsyth, op. cit., p. 22.

[3] R. Roberts, *The Preacher as Man of Letters,* p. 47.

at the best a skilful conflation and at the worst a patchwork quilt. However polished and logical, it will lack the power and conviction of truth personally appropriated, a synthesis fused in the crucible of the preacher's mind and soul.

Indirect preparation consists therefore of the continual cultivation of the preacher's own mental and spiritual life. A great musician—was it Paderewski?—once said that if ever he missed practising for a day, he knew it; if he missed two days, his friends knew it; if he missed three days, the public knew it. What practice is to the musician, prayer and study are to the preacher: he neglects either at his peril. Activism is a deadly snare. It is fatally easy for the modern minister to be running hither and thither full of good works and have no time left for the secret place of the Most High. *Laborare est orare* contains just sufficient truth to make it a very dangerous half-truth. It was said of John Henry Newman that when he ascended the pulpit stairs men felt that he had come straight from the presence of God.[1] After he had communed with God in the mount, the face of Moses shone. There is no mistaking the minister who is a man of prayer. 'The inner radiance of intimate fellowship with God is a thing that you can never counterfeit; and those who themselves know God will know infallibly whether you have it or not.'[2] The Anglican minister is in duty bound to read the offices of Morning and Evening

1 See Principal Shairp's description of Newman at St. Mary's: 'The look and bearing of the preacher were as of one who dwelt apart, who, though he knew his age well, did not live in it. From the seclusion of study, and abstinence, and prayer, from habitual dwelling with the unseen, he seemed to come forth that one day of the week to speak to others of the things he had seen and known.' W. Ward, *Life of Newman*, i. 65.

2 Stephen Neill, *On the Ministry*, p. 31.

Prayer every day, privately if not publicly. He is pledged to *at least* this daily discipline of devotion. Free Church ministers whose Churches do not provide them with such a daily discipline must provide one for themselves if their ministry is to be effective under God. And they could do worse than make the Prayer Book offices the basis of their daily prayers.[1]

Next to the maintenance of the minister's own devotional life stands the apostolic injunction: 'Give attendance to reading' (1 Tim. iv. 13). The preacher must never cease to be a student: the study is the most important room of the Manse. The old rule that a minister should spend four hours in his study every morning still holds if he is to bring forth out of his treasure things new and old. No man can sustain an effective pulpit ministry unless he keep his mind fresh and well-stored. And that can only be done through regular systematic reading which is both broad and deep. There is no other way. The Bible, it should be needless to say, must always have priority among the minister's books. 'Other books he uses, but on this he lives his corporate life. It is what integrates him into the Church of all ages.'[2] 'Some preachers know it only in the way of business, as a sermon quarry. But the true ministry must live on it.'[3] Books about the Bible can never be a substitute for the study of Holy Scripture itself. The writer well remembers being introduced, as a young theological student, to Dr. Campbell Morgan in the vestry of Westminster Chapel after an evening service. Morgan had just held a crowded church

1 This at least ensures the reading through of the Psalter every month, the greater part of the Old Testament once a year, and the whole of the New Testament twice a year.

2 P. T. Forsyth, op. cit., p. 9.

3 ibid., p. 38.

for three-quarters of an hour with a massive exposition. With all the audacity of youth I asked him what was the secret of his success in the ministry. I can see him now shaking his white forelock as he almost exploded with: 'No man can tell that!' He then went on to tell me how, as a young man of twenty-two, he had come out of what he described as a perfect intellectual fog and shut himself up for a year with his Bible. It was because he lived on his Bible that Campbell Morgan was able to expound it with such power.

The preacher should not be content with a study of Holy Scripture which is limited to the English Bible. Part of it, at least, should be occupied with the Hebrew and Greek texts; and the more the better. No translation, however accurate, can ever take the place of a first-hand acquaintance with a document in the language in which it was written. F. B. Meyer once told a meeting of ministers in Brisbane that he had made it a rule of his ministry to spend an hour each morning with his Hebrew Old Testament and another hour reading the New Testament in Greek.

After the Bible the great devotional literature of Christendom should be frequently to hand. No man who is called to preach can afford to neglect Bunyan and Doddridge, Thomas à Kempis and St. John of the Cross. Theology also should have a foremost place. The minister, as Daniel Jenkins reminds us, is the representative in the local church of the great Church: part of his function is 'to enable the local church to look at itself and its vocation in the setting of the whole purpose of God for all His people.'[1] Only a thorough grasp of systematic theology will enable him to do this. Again, since the preacher must know the world of men

[1] *Congregationalism: A Restatement*, p. 77.

to which he has to preach, he will find the study of history, biography and literature particularly rewarding. Indeed, everything that a minister reads will be grist to his mill. The more informed he is, the better will he be able in his preaching to 'contemporize' the everlasting Gospel with which he is put in trust.

Indirect preparation for preaching is not confined to the study, however. It is as large as life and as broad as experience. 'When you sit down in your study to write a sermon,' says James S. Stewart, 'you are not without vital resources behind you. All your experience of God, all your acquaintance with life, all your knowledge of men, all your fellowship with the great minds of the centuries, will come in then to your aid.'[1] The work of the study needs therefore to be supplemented by the acquaintance with life and knowledge of men which comes through personal contact between minister and people. Bishop Stephen Neill likens preaching to weaving. 'There are the two factors of the warp and the woof. There is the fixed, unalterable element, which for us is the Word of God; there is the variable element, which enables the weaver to change and vary the pattern at his will. For us that variable element is the constantly changing pattern of people and of situations.'[2] The proper study of mankind is man: regular pastoral work is therefore indispensable for effective preaching. To set the two in antithesis is quite wrong; they are complementary. The preaching which grips men and women because it speaks to their condition is not that of the minister who neglects pastoral visitation under the pretext that he cannot give to his people both his head and his heels. It is only by close daily contact

[1] op. cit., p. 105.

[2] op. cit., p. 74.

with his flock, by sitting where they sit, that the minister can discern their real needs and difficulties, their problems and temptations, their hopes and their fears. And it is out of such pastoral contacts that effective preaching grows. This close inter-relationship of preaching and pastoral work is emphasized by H. H. Farmer in his admirable Warrack Lectures:[1]

> The act of preaching is part of a larger system of personal relationships and cannot be rightly understood in separation from it. . . . It is part of a pastoral relationship, one activity of a settled and continuous ministry. . . . Those who have what are called 'pulpit gifts' will suffer great loss of power if their preaching is not surrounded by those more direct and intimate personal relations which are part of a faithful pastoral ministry exercised over a number of years.

To emphasize the importance of indirect preparation for preaching is not to belittle direct preparation. Both are necessary and one is the complement of the other. How, then, should the preacher set about making a sermon? Where does he begin? What will be the successive stages of his work?

Before considering these questions, it will be well to recall the clearly-defined psychological stages which underlie all creative work. There are four: 1. *Preparation*—the initial stage in which material is collected. As Goethe says, if you keep on piling up wood it will one day catch fire. This is the stage at which the 'wood' is gathered together. 2. *Incubation*. After the material has been collected, some time must elapse before it can profitably be worked upon. During this period the unconscious mind is sorting it out and making its own synthesis of what is relevant. This stage of seem-

[1] op. cit., pp. 93-94.

ing inactivity may be relatively long or short, but it is vital in all creative work. 3. *Inspiration* is the stage at which the particular work takes shape; the wood catches fire. It should proceed without interruption until the work is complete. 4. *Criticism* is the final stage in which the completed work is examined objectively and critically. Lack of balance is adjusted, mistakes are rectified, and the work as a whole is pruned and polished.

The application to homiletics is obvious. The fact that the preacher has to have his sermons ready for Sunday makes it advisable for him to begin them early enough in the week to allow sufficient time for each of these stages, and particularly for the second—the stage of incubation. In practice, this means that the preliminary work on Sunday morning's sermon should begin not later than the previous Tuesday morning. After waiting upon God, the minister selects the text from which he feels led to preach; commentaries and lexicons are consulted; notes are made on points of background, exegesis, application, and any other relevant matter. This completes the first stage: the particular material for this sermon has been gathered. The minister may now put his notes on one side and turn his attention to similar preparation for the evening sermon. To allow for the period of incubation, a day or two should elapse between this preliminary work and the actual writing of each sermon, or the preparation of final notes if the sermon is not to be written out in full. Once begun, the sermon should be written quickly, preferably at one sitting. It will be advisable to go through it later with the blue pencil and parts may have to be re-written; but this is a separate and *final* stage. Any attempt to be self-critical during the actual writing will only inhibit the creative faculties.

Two things must be clear in the preacher's mind when he begins the preparation of a sermon—his theme and his aim. Rousseau tells us that the way to write a love-letter is to begin by not knowing what you are going to say and end by not knowing what you have said. Some sermons give the impression of having been written in precisely that way. Like rivers that wander through the desert and finally get lost in the sand, they lead nowhere. One great advantage of preaching from a text—assuming that the sermon really is an exposition of it—is that the text both provides the theme and indicates the lines along which it may be developed. It sets the course of the sermon and limits the preacher to certain aspects of his subject. Expository preaching of this kind is clear-cut and well defined; it avoids vagueness and discoursiveness. A proper balance in the selection of subjects is best maintained by following the Christian Year. 'The great landmarks of the Christian Year—Advent, Christmas, Lent, Good Friday, Easter, Whitsunday, Trinity—set us our course, and suggest our basic themes. They compel us to keep close to the fundamental doctrines of the faith. They summon us back from the bypaths where we might be prone to linger, to the great highway of redemption. They ensure that in our preaching we shall constantly be returning to those mighty acts of God which the Church exists to declare.'[1]

Not only must the preacher, from the very beginning, be quite clear as to what his sermon is to be about; he must also know precisely what he desires it to achieve. One of the first principles of education is that a teacher preparing his lesson notes must begin by stating his aim: What, he must ask, does this particular lesson set out to do? The effective

[1] J. S. Stewart, op. cit., p. 111.

preacher begins in the same way. A sermon which aims at nothing usually achieves its objective. The preacher must preach for a verdict. The inter-relationship of theme and aim is well expressed by H. H. Farmer: 'Our preaching,' he says, 'has got to be strongly doctrinal, not in the manner of the theological lecture room, but in such wise that doctrine and life are seen to be inseparably bound up together.'[1]

When the theme and aim of a sermon have been clearly defined, there remain four distinct stages in dealing with the text. First comes the stage of criticism: the text should be carefully examined—preferably in the original Hebrew or Greek—in the light of all that the best biblical scholarship has to say about it. Any variant readings should be compared and an attempt made to ascertain its original form and correct historical setting. It will be useful and instructive at this stage to compare the renderings of the text in different translations—the Authorized Version, the Revised Version (especially the margin), the Revised Standard Version, Moffatt, and Knox. The next stage is exegesis. Here the best exegetical commentaries—ancient and modern—are indispensable. Luther, Calvin and Matthew Henry should be consulted alongside of George Adam Smith and Skinner, Vincent Taylor and Dodd. Before the words of Isaiah or St. Paul can be interpreted for the present day, it is necessary to know what they meant for those who first heard them. These two initial stages, it must be emphasized, are fundamental: they provide the only sound basis of preaching. An otherwise excellent sermon may be completely invalidated by faulty exegesis. After exegesis comes theological interpretation: this particular passages of Scripture must be set in its larger theological context and seen in the

op. cit., p. 143.

light of the biblical revelation as a whole. It is not sufficient to have ascertained the original significance of some words of Isaiah, for instance; the preacher must go on to ask what they mean *in the Christian perspective*. The Old Testament is to be interpreted not merely as Hebrew literature but as Christian Scripture. It means for us what it has come to mean in the light of Christ and His Cross. Similarly, the strange, and to us remote, language of blood sacrifice in which the New Testament writers describe the Work of Christ derives its content from the sacrificial worship of the Old Testament of which the Cross is the 'fulfilment.' For all Christian preaching the Cross is crucial: the key to all the Scriptures is Christ.[1] The final stage is the practical application of the text to the condition and needs of the hearers. Preaching is not preaching unless it 'contemporizes' the Gospel. The Word of God contained in words spoken by Isaiah to a pastoral community in the eighth century B.C. must be related to the vastly different conditions of Western society at the beginning of the atomic age in the twentieth century A.D. What, the preacher must ask, is the relevance of these words of a Hebrew prophet for the problems precipitated by automation or the 'credit squeeze'? What Word of God do they speak to John Smith the grocer and David Jones the solicitor, Mary Jackson the housewife and Pat Green the typist as they sit over there in the back pew?

The sermon itself need not traverse these successive stages, of course; but the preacher must. And he should remember that the real meaning of a text may be quite different from that suggested by a superficial reading of it in an English translation. The preacher should therefore make a careful

[1] The 'Torch Bible Commentaries' (S.C.M.) aim at giving a theological interpretation of each book in the setting of the biblical revelation as a whole.

study of the key words in the passage which he is to expound. This brings us back to the desirability of reading the sacred text in the original Hebrew and Greek. Not every minister, however, has sufficient facility in the biblical languages to do this with profit. In that case, Young's *Analytical Concordance* is an indispensable guide. Indeed, even those who have a good working knowledge of Hebrew and Greek will find great assistance in its comprehensive classification of biblical words. The theological significance of leading terms is admirably summarized in *A Theological Word Book of the Bible* (ed. Alan Richardson)—a book which no minister should be without.

Two passages, one from the Old Testament and one from the New, will serve to illustrate the importance of such a study of biblical words:

1. Prov. xxix. 18, 'Where there is no vision, the people perish,' appears to mean merely that no community can survive without foresight, breadth of outlook, sound judgment. The real meaning, however, is quite different. The Hebrew word translated 'vision' (*ḥāzôn*) has a revelatory content: it is the term used for the vision of a prophet. And the verb rendered 'perish' (*pāraʿ*) conveys the idea of loosening and hence disintegration. The passage may therefore be paraphrased thus: 'Where there is no living revelation, no perceived contact between God and man, the ties which hold society together are loosed and finally broken.' In short: Without religion, social disintegration.

2. Jn. viii. 51, 'If a man keep my saying, he shall never see death,' is enigmatic enough until the real meaning of the Greek verbs is seen. The verb translated 'keep' (*tēreō*) means to watch or observe, and the other verb *theōreō*,

which is rendered 'see,' implies special attention, noticing as a matter of interest. Once this is realized, the meaning becomes clear. 'The Lord does not promise that anyone who keeps His word shall avoid the physical incident called death; but that if his mind is turned towards that word it will not pay any attention to death; death will be to it irrelevant.'[1]

The most thorough preparation of this kind is essential if the preacher is to be a workman that needeth not to be ashamed, rightly dividing the word of truth. Those who shirk it join what Phillips Brooks calls 'the race of clerical visionaries who think vast, dim, vague thoughts, and do no work.'[2] It is not such who preach with power. Was it Quiller-Couch who said that only out of long preparation can come the truly triumphant flash? No less care is needed in the actual writing of the sermon if it is to be an effective instrument for the Spirit of God. Writing a sermon is quite different from writing an essay: the former is intended to be *spoken;* the latter read. When the preacher writes his sermon, therefore, it is the *spoken* word, in all its concreteness and directness, which he has to transcribe on to his manuscript. And not only the spoken word, but the *preached* word. Hence the minister must write from the pulpit, as it were. 'When you sit down to write in your study,' says James Stewart, 'you must visualize a gathered congregation.' This 'will keep the dominant notes of urgency and reality, of appeal for a verdict, sounding unmistakably.'[3] The late H. C. Carter, who for thirty-four years exercised such a powerful ministry at Emmanuel Congregational Church,

1 W. Temple, *Readings in St. John's Gospel* (First Series), p. 147.

2 *Lectures on Preaching,* p. 88.

3 op. cit., p. 119.

Cambridge, was once asked by a theological student how he managed to maintain the direct, personal note so consistently in his preaching. He replied that when he sat down to write a sermon, he tried to imagine that he was writing a letter to a friend.

'It is, I think, a capital error, which many make,' says H. H. Farmer, 'to suppose that when a sermon has been written, it is ready. It is not. The writing is merely preliminary. As sermon, indeed, it does not at that stage exist at all. It is merely manuscript. The important thing is to re-absorb it, through your own person, into the context of God's saving purpose, so that it ceases to be a composition lying there on the desk, an "it," and becomes part of you as a person, one soon to be a "thou," God's "thou," to another "I." '[1] The preacher must possess the sermon and the sermon must possess the preacher before it can be truly preached.

We have considered the craftsmanship of preaching at some length. It is not to be belittled. The divine Word is worthy of the finest instrument that it is within our power to provide. To offer anything less comes perilously near to blasphemy. But craftsmanship alone will not produce preaching. There may be craftsmanship without preaching, just as there may be preaching without craftsmanship. The wind bloweth where it listeth. 'It is one thing to learn the technique and mechanics of preaching: it is quite another to preach a sermon which will draw back the veil and make the barriers fall that hide the face of God.'[2] That is the function of the preached Word in worship. 'The sermon is divinely intended to be one of those high places of the spirit where men and women grow piercingly aware of the

[1] op. cit., pp. 32-33.

[2] J. S. Stewart, op. cit., p. 101.

eternal, and where a worshipping congregation—forgetting all about the preacher—sees "no man, save Jesus only".'[1]

But preaching has also a Godward reference. It is not only prophetic; it is also confessional. Here revelation and response, *Wort* and *Antwort,* become luminous in their fusion. 'The sermon,' says Forsyth, 'is the Word of the Gospel returning in confesion to God who gave it. It is addressed to men indeed, but in truth it is offered to God.'[2]

[1] ibid., p. 72. Cf. Ian Maclaren's description of John Carmichael's first sermon at Drumtochty: 'I never realized the unseen world as I did that day in the Free Kirk of Drumtochty. . . . The subject was Jesus Christ, and before he had spoken five minutes I was convinced that Christ was present. The preacher faded from before one's eyes, and there rose the figure of the Nazarene. . . . His voice might be heard any moment, as I have imagined it in my lonely hours by the winter fire or on the solitary hills . . . "Come unto Me . . . and I will give you rest." ' *Beside the Bonnie Brier Bush,* pp. 96-98.

[2] op. cit., p. 97.

CHAPTER IV

Public Prayer

In the old Sharrow Cemetery at Sheffield stands a monument to the City's poet, James Montgomery. Inscribed on its four sides is the full text of his great hymn on prayer:

> . . . the Christian's vital breath,
> The Christian's native air.

Prayer is certainly the vital breath and native air of Christian worship. All its basic principles come to a burning focus here. Worship, as we have seen, depends upon revelation, it is essentially the Church's response to God's Word; and the vehicles of that response are prayer and praise. Again, worship springs from the activity of the Holy Spirit who indwells the Church; and it is the Spirit's prompting which is the fount of true prayer.[1] Again, worship is an indefeasibly corporate activity, the offering of the whole Church as the Body of Christ; and prayer, as Daniel Jenkins reminds us,[2] is primarily a corporate act, individual prayer being supplementary to the commerce with God of the People of God. Again, worship is the indispensable prerequisite of effective Christian witness; and prayer is a 'means of grace' through which the Church's strength is renewed.

I PRIVATE AND CORPORATE PRAYER

Free Church worship is frequently vitiated by two com-

[1] See Rom. viii. 26.

[2] See *Prayer and the Service of God,* ch. vii.

mon confusions. First, there is the confusion between private and corporate prayer, a legacy of nineteenth-century atomistic individualism which destroys the essentially corporate nature of Christian worship. Worship is a united act; it is not the sum-total of a number of concurrent individual acts of devotion. The private prayers of Mary Jones, Tom Smith, Robert Brown and Anne Johnson do not constitute an act of worship just because they happen to be sitting together in the same church at the same hour; nor does the fact that they may be listening to another person—the minister—saying his own prayers aloud.[1]

About this latter point more must be said. One of the most common mistakes which results from this confusion between private and corporate prayer is that the leader of the worship—be he minister or layman—offers his own prayers instead of leading the prayers of the Church. Perhaps the place where this is most common—and fatal—is the Sunday School. How many Sunday School superintendents and leaders of departments succeed in *leading* the children in prayer? More often he (or she) prays *over* them, offering, maybe in moving language and with evident sincerity, a prayer admirable enough as private petition but quite inept as the *children's* prayer. Small wonder that the boys and girls resort to amusing themselves by their own devices until the leader's exercise is ended. This confusion, however, is by no means confined to the Sunday School; it is exemplified in the all-too-common pulpit monologue to which congregations have to listen instead of uniting in a

[1] See J. E. Rattenbury, *Vital Elements of Public Worship*, pp. 90-91: 'What is helpful in private devotion may be a hindrance in public religious services. . . . Public worship is not just a multitude of acts of the various individuals who make up a congregation. Whatever the individual contributes, the public act of worship is corporate.'

corporate act of prayer. A friend once remarked to the writer concerning a certain popular preacher, 'People would come for miles to hear him pray.' If that meant that by so doing they themselves were led in prayer, so be it; but did it mean that?

A further result of this confusion is that *in fact* the minister's monologue is frequently addressed to the congregation instead of to God. What purports to be prayer may degenerate into a subtle haranguing of the people or at best a display of pious oratory intended for their edification. The American newspaper reporter who ironically commended 'the best prayer ever offered to a Boston audience' said more than he knew.

In corporate worship it is the congregation that prays. Public prayer, rightly understood, is not the sum-total of individual prayers; nor is it the passive attention to the minister's private prayer; it is *common prayer*, the prayer of the People of God. It is the minister's duty and privilege, not just himself to pray, but to lead a corporate act of prayer. His purpose is the same whether he uses a set form or prays *ex tempore:* he offers, on behalf of his people, the prayers of the whole congregation.

II DIFFERENT TYPES OF PRAYER

The second common confusion results from failure to distinguish between clearly defined types of prayer, all of which have a proper place in a full act of worship. Nine such may be listed:

1. *Adoration*. This essential part of public prayer strikes the key-note of all true worship—the humble recognition of

God as God; the giving unto the Lord of the glory due unto His name. 'Adoration is the contemplative surrender to a supreme good.'[1] It is exemplified in Faber's great hymn: 'My God, how wonderful Thou art.' In the prayer of adoration there is no petition:

> . . . we ask for nought,
> But simply worship Thee.

It expresses the proper attitude of the creature in the presence of the Creator, the glad submission of the heart

> That gives Thee glory, love, and praise
> For being what Thou art.

The prayer of adoration thus gives to worship objectivity: God, and not our own feelings, is its focal centre. Two prayers of this type will serve as illustrations:[2]

Great is thy name, O Lord, and greatly to be praised, and to be had in reverence of all them that call upon thee. For thou only art God; we are the people of thy pasture and the sheep of thy hand. Therefore we worship and adore thee, Father, Son and Holy Ghost, ever one God, world without end. Amen.

O thou who art beyond our sight, above our thought, infinite, eternal, and unchangeable: thy wisdom shines in all thy works; thy glory is shown in thy goodness to men; and thy grace and truth are revealed in Christ. Therefore we adore thee, our Father and our God, for ever and ever. Amen.

The prayer of adoration is sometimes combined with the second type, Invocation, to which we now turn.

2. *Invocation,* as the name implies, is a prayer calling upon God to assist us in the worship that we offer. Along

[1] F. Heiler, *Prayer,* p. 360.

[2] The first prayer is my own; the second is taken from 'Prayers of Adoration' in *A Book of Public Worship,* p. 83.

with Adoration therefore, its rightful place is in the Prayers of Approach at the beginning of the service. Many of the classic collects provide admirable models:

Almighty God, unto whom all hearts be open, all desires known, and from whom no secrets are hid: Cleanse the thoughts of our hearts by the inspiration of thy Holy Spirit, that we may perfectly love thee, and worthily magnify thy holy name; through Jesus Christ our Lord. Amen.

O God, forasmuch as without thee we are not able to please thee; Mercifully grant that thy Holy Spirit may in all things direct and rule our hearts; through Jesus Christ our Lord. Amen.

3. *Confession.* The rhythm of the Christian life is repentance and renewal. The Confession of Sins is therefore a necessary element in a full act of worship, and its normal place, as a Prayer of Approach, is early in the service, usually following the opening act of praise. As a common act of penitence it should be sufficiently general for the congregation to make it their own. There is no better pattern than the General Confession from the *Book of Common Prayer:*[1]

Almighty and most merciful Father; we have erred and strayed from thy ways like lost sheep. We have followed too much the devices and desires of our own hearts. We have offended against thy holy laws. We have left undone those things which we ought to have done; and we have done those things which we ought not to have done; and there is no health in us. But thou, O Lord, have mercy upon us, miserable

[1] The General Confession should be used in its full classic form. It is mutilated in some service books by the omission of phrases which were offensive to 'liberal modernism,' viz. 'and there is no health in us' and 'miserable offenders.' For a penetrating commentary on this great prayer see D. R. Davies, *Down Peacock's Feathers.*

offenders. Spare thou them, O God, which confess their faults. Restore thou them that are penitent; according to thy promises declared unto mankind in Christ Jesu our Lord. And grant, O most merciful Father, for his sake; that we may hereafter live a godly, righteous, and sober life, to the glory of thy holy name. Amen.

Along with the actual confession of sins go petition for pardon and supplication for grace, and the prayer should be followed by some form of Absolution or a scriptural Assurance of Pardon.

4. *Thanksgiving* is the natural response of the worshipping congregation to the declaration (in sermon, or sacrament, or Gospel reading) of the Gospel of God's grace in Jesus Christ. It is thus one of the characteristic notes of Christian worship, giving its name, as it does, to the central service, the Eucharist,[1] in which it is the key-note of the great Consecration Prayer.[2] The General Thanksgiving is a model for this type of prayer:

Almighty God, Father of all mercies, we thine unworthy servants do give thee most humble and hearty thanks for all thy goodness and loving kindness to us, and to all men. We bless thee for our creation, preservation, and all the blessings of this life; but above all for thine inestimable love in the redemption of the world by our Lord Jesus Christ; for the means of grace, and for the hope of glory. And, we beseech thee, give us that due sense of all thy mercies, that our hearts may be unfeignedly thankful, and that we shew forth thy praise, not only with our lips, but in our lives; by giving up ourselves to thy service, and by walking before thee in holiness and righteousness all our days; through Jesus Christ our Lord, to whom with thee and the Holy Ghost be all honour and glory, world without end. Amen.

[1] From *eucharisteō* = I give thanks.

[2] See pp. 163-174.

Note the ascending sequence: 'We bless thee for our creation, preservation, and all the blessings of this life; *but above all* for thine inestimable love in the redemption of the world by our Lord Jesus Christ.' Thanksgiving for redemption should always be the climax and focal point of the Prayer of Thanksgiving.

5. *Supplication* and the next kind of prayer, Intercession, are prayers of petition in which we make our requests known unto God. The distinction between them is that one is subjective and the other objective. Whereas in Intercession we are concerned with the needs of all sorts and conditions of men, Supplication is essentially prayer for our own needs; a distinction which should not be overlooked. The Prayer of Supplication, therefore, along with the Confession of Sins, supplies the subjective element which is the complement of the objective in properly balanced worship. Here, obviously, there is room for a great variety of expression including prayer for special graces, i.e. faithfulness, love, obedience, trust, guidance, peace. An example of general Supplication may be quoted from *A Book of Public Worship:*[1]

Holy Father, who hast redeemed us with the precious blood of thy dear Son; keep us, we beseech thee, steadfast in faith, and enable us to live no longer unto ourselves, but unto him who died for us and rose again. Strengthen us by thy grace that we may fight the good fight, and finish our course, and keep the faith. Help us manfully to overcome our temptations, and faithfully to fulfil the work thou hast given us to do. Shed abroad thy love in our hearts; make us kind one to another, tender-hearted, forgiving one another, even as thou for Christ's sake hast forgiven us; and persuade us that neither death nor life, nor things present nor things to come, shall be

[1] First Order of Service, p. 5.

able to separate us from thy love, which is in Christ Jesus our Lord. Amen.

Supplication may fittingly follow either Confession and Absolution or Thanksgiving.

6. *Intercession.* The Prayer of Intercession may take several forms. It may be the traditional 'long' prayer in which petitions for the Church, the Queen, the British Nation and Commonwealth, the sick, the bereaved, the lonely and sad, etc., follow in an orderly but closely-woven sequence. Or it may be broken up into a number of short prayers each concluding with a versicle and response[1] or simply with the people's Amen. Or again, it may take the form of a 'bidding' prayer in which the minister bids the congregation pray for the subjects of intercession, a short period of silence following each bidding. For example:[2]

Let us pray:

For the whole Church of God, that in every land it may be kept faithful, and throughout the world remain one in Christ Jesus.

For the churches of our own order, that preserving their liberty in bondage to Christ, they may promote the good of his whole body, and serve their generation in uprightness and truth.

For all kings and rulers of men, that they may govern in righteousness and justice, and rule only to serve.

For our own Queen and the Royal Family, that they may be blessed with all princely virtues, and preserved to eternal life.

[1] E.g. *Minister:* Lord, hear our prayer;
People: And let our cry come unto thee.

[2] These biddings are selected from General Intercessions XI in *A Book of Public Worship,* in which examples of each form of Intercession are to be found.

For the Government now in office, and for the High Court of Parliament, that our laws may be just and our politics pure, and that goodwill may everywhere prevail.

For our industrial and social life, that our commerce be honest, our industry humane, our people upright, and our progress free from bitterness.

For all who teach and all who learn, that wisdom may inform knowledge, and the light of God's truth make us wise.

For all who suffer : the poor, that their necessities be relieved; the sick, that they be restored to health; the tempted, that they be strengthened; the fallen, that they repent; the prisoners, that they be reclaimed; and the persecuted, that they be delivered.

For the dying, that they may rise to eternal life; and for the departed, that they may rest in peace.

For all who are near and dear to us, that we may live to serve and love each other, and find our bond in Christ.

The Intercessions may then conclude with a prayer such as this:

Heavenly Father, who hast promised faithfully to fulfil those things that we ask believingly in the name of thy dear Son; accept, we beseech thee, our petitions, and fulfil them, not as we ask in our ignorance and unworthiness, nor as we deserve in our sinfulness, but as thou knowest and lovest us in Jesus Christ, thy Son, our Lord. Amen.

7. *Commemoration of the Faithful Departed.* In worship there is realized, as nowhere else, the communion of saints: the local church becomes one with the whole Church, militant on earth and triumphant in heaven.

> One family we dwell in Him,
>   One Church, above, beneath,
> Though now divided by the stream,
>   The narrow stream of death;

One army of the Living God,
  To His command we bow;
Part of His host hath crossed the flood,
  And part is crossing now.

It is fitting therefore that this realization should find expression in the structure of the service by a conscious act of grateful remembrance of those who have departed this life to be with Christ. Its place is clearly at the end of the Intercessions in which the Church Militant has been remembered before God. It may well form the conclusion of the 'long' intercessory prayer; or it make take the form of a separate short prayer immediately following it:

O God, before whose face the generations rise and pass away; the strength of those who labour and suffer, and the repose of the holy and blessed dead: We rejoice in the communion of thy saints. We remember all who have faithfully lived; all who have peacefully died, and especially those most dear to us. Lift us into light and love; and give us at last our portion with those who have trusted in thee, and striven in all things to do thy holy will. And unto thy name, with the Church on earth and the Church in heaven, would we ascribe all honour and glory, world without end. Amen.[1]

8. *Illumination*. In Calvin's Genevan order of service the preaching of the Word was preceded by a Prayer for Illumination, a practice which has become traditional in the Reformed Churches. This prayer is a brief invocation of the Holy Spirit (parallel to the *Epiclesis* in the Consecration Prayer of the Eucharist) to make effective the declaration of the Gospel in the hearts and lives of the hearers. It is a clear indication of the 'sacramental' view of preaching (which takes the place of the Elevation of the Host in the

[1] From *The Book of Common Order* of the United Church of Canada, p. 19.

Mass) in the Reformed tradition, as the following example shows:[1]

O God, who hast called us unto thy kingdom and glory by Christ Jesus; let thy Gospel come unto us not in word only, but also in power and in the Holy Ghost, that it may be spoken and heard not as the word of men but as thy Word, which effectually worketh in all who believe: through Jesus Christ our Lord. Amen.

9. *Oblation* is the climax of corporate prayer. It is the Body of Christ, in union with its Risen Head, offering itself through the power of the Spirit to the Father. Its proper position is at the end of the Consecration Prayer[2] in the service of Holy Communion where it takes the place of the Great Oblation (i.e. the solemn offering in memorial before God of the consecrated elements as the body and blood of Christ) of the Mass:

And here we offer and present unto Thee ourselves, our souls and bodies, to be a reasonable, holy, and living sacrifice; and we beseech Thee mercifully to accept this our sacrifice of praise and thanksgiving, as, in fellowship with all the faithful in heaven and on earth, we pray Thee to fulfil in us, and in all men, the purpose of Thy redeeming love; through Jesus Christ our Lord, by whom, and with whom, in the unity of the Holy Spirit, all honour and glory be unto Thee, O Father Almighty, world without end. Amen.[3]

When there is no celebration of the Lord's Supper, a Prayer of Oblation may fittingly be used to dedicate the offerings of the people:

[1] From *A Book of Public Worship,* First Order of Service, p. 7.

[2] In the Communion Office of *The Book of Common Prayer,* the Prayer of Oblation follows the Lord's Prayer immediately after the reception of the elements. See chapter II, p. 31.

[3] From *The Book of Common Order* of the Church of Scotland, p. 120.

We are thine, O Lord; all that we have is thine; and of thine own have we given unto thee. Accept, we beseech thee, the offerings of thy people, the symbols of our toil and thy blessing; since with them we offer and present unto thee ourselves, our souls and bodies, to be a reasonable, holy, and living sacrifice; through him who loved us and gave himself for us, even Jesus Christ our Lord. Amen.[1]

This corresponds to the Lesser Oblation (i.e. the Offertory) of the Mass.

Before considering in detail the place of each type of prayer in the structure of a service, the necessity of properly ordered prayer must be emphasized. Whether he selects set prayers, writes his own prayers, or (more especially) uses extemporary prayer, the minister must avoid confusing these distinct types if he is to lead worship effectively. There is a tendency, all too common, to 'jump about' from say Invocation to Intercession, then to Thanksgiving with perhaps a touch of Confession, then back again to Thanksgiving with more Intercession. This makes it extraordinarily difficult for the congregation to follow the minister's thought and make the prayer their own. If their minds, like Christopher Robin's, keep flying off at a tangent, they are scarcely to be blamed. Moreover, vital elements of a complete act of worship (e.g. Adoration and Confession) may not be given their full place, or may even be omitted altogether. There is no merit in disorderly worship; it is confusing for men and dishonouring to God. Our God is a God of order, not of confusion.

III THE ORDERING OF PRAYER

The various parts of a service of worship—hymns, prayers, scripture readings, sermon—are not so many 'items' in

[1] This prayer is mine.

a programme; they are elements which together constitute an organic whole.[1] Classic Christian worship, Eastern and Western, Catholic and Reformed, has a certain basic structure derived from the Bible and the practice of the Apostolic Church. Its central act, as we have seen, is the Eucharist in which the Ministry of the Word leads up to the sacramental fellowship of the Lord's Supper. We turn now to examine this basic structure of worship more closely. What is its significance? To what end does it lead? And what are its practical implications for the ordering of a service?

First then, Christian worship is essentially drama. It is the dramatic representation of the whole relationship of God to man in creation, redemption, and final consummation. Just as the human embryo in the womb recapitulates the physical development of the race, so in each full act of worship there is a recapitulation of man's spiritual history in the setting of the eternal purpose and redeeming activity of God. The traditional Call to Worship with which the Reformed service begins takes us back to the Creation, reminding us as it does of the primal relationship between God and man: 'Our help is in the name of the Lord, who made heaven and earth.' This is also set forth in the opening act of praise of which William Kethe's paraphrase of the hundreth Psalm is typical:

> The Lord ye know is God indeed;
> Without our aid He did us make;
> We are His folk, He doth us feed;
> And for His sheep He doth us take.

There you have man made in the image of God, made for fellowship with God, yet a creature entirely dependent upon God.

[1] T. L. Harris aptly describes a service consisting of unrelated 'items' as 'a kind of sacred vaudeville.' See *Christian Public Worship,* pp. 63f.

What comes next in the biblical story? The Fall. Man in his rebellion repudiates his creatureliness. Not only is he made in the image of God; he is also a sinner, a rebel who forfeits his Paradise of communion with God. And so there follows the Confession of Sins. Man (Adam) acknowledges his fallen state:

We have erred and strayed from thy ways like lost sheep. We have followed too much the devices and desires of our own hearts. We have offended against thy holy laws. We have left undone those things which we ought to have done; and we have done those things which we ought not to have done; and there is no health in us.

But the Creator is also the Redeemer. Man's helpless predicament is met by God's saving grace. 'He hath not dealt with us after our sins; nor rewarded us according to our iniquities.' The story of God's saving acts, as they are unfolded in the Scriptures of the Old and New Testaments, is therefore read; culminating in the Incarnation, the Cross, and the Empty Tomb.

A second Adam to the fight
And to the rescue came.

Not only, however, has God acted in the past for us men and for our salvation; 'it is the potency of His past actions in the present that constitutes the news of the Bible as the good news of the Gospel.'[1] The reading of the Old and New Testaments is therefore followed by the sermon which is intended to 'contemporize' the Gospel, relating the redemptive action of God which the Bible declares to the needs of men and women in the modern world.

With what result? Fallen man becomes redeemed man:

[1] John Marsh in *Ways of Worship,* ch. iv, 'Congregationalist,' p. 154, to whom I am deeply indebted in this section.

Paradise Lost becomes Paradise Regained. The divine intention in Creation, fellowship between man and God, is restored; and in that new relationship with God man finds himself brought into a new relationship with his fellow man. Thus the sermon is followed by a fellowship of prayer in which Intercession and Thanksgiving lead to the moment of vision at the Table of the Lord. Here in the Sacrament of Holy Communion time is transcended; past and present are taken up into the future consummation; man, fallen yet redeemed, is translated into the eternal world and tastes of the powers of the age to come.

The descent from the mountain top to the plain marks the end of worship. After a final hymn the congregation is dismissed with the Blessing. 'So the believer, who came from a world in which he is committed to a ceaseless struggle with sin, is sent back to it and to its warfare having been confronted with the picture of himself as God sees him, with the story of what God has done to save him, and with the assurance, in sermon and benediction, that the God who promises His succour will not fail to provide it.'[1]

The shape of the basic structure of worship emerges more clearly from this consideration of its dramatic significance. Three distinct stages are discernible; and they correspond to the three stages on the road of Christian mysticism —Purgation, Illumination, and Union.[2] The first stage is the Approach in praise and prayer. Here the worshipper sees himself for what he is—a creature made for communion with God, yet a sinner alienated from God; and he acknowledges his utter dependence upon God for restoration and

[1] Marsh, op. cit., p. 153.

[2] See C. F. Miller, *Prayers for Parish Worship*, Introduction, pp. vii-xiii.

life. This corresponds to the mystic's stage of Purgation. The second stage is the Ministry of the Word in Scripture and Sermon. The light of the glorious Gospel of the blessed God breaks into the darkness of man's fallen world. Where sin abounds, grace does much more abound. The stage of Illumination is reached. Finally, through the grace of the Gospel the worshipper is brought to the stage of Fellowship in prayer and sacrament. The goal of all worship, Union with God, has been attained.

The arrangement and sequence of the constituent parts of these three successive stages of worship represent a two-fold movement in the mind and spirit of the worshipper. First, there is an alternate movement from God to man and from man to God: God calls and man responds. There is, as it were, a dialogue between God and His worshipping Church. The worshipper moves rhythmically from vision to response, and thence to fresh vision and new response.[1] The typical Reformed service begins with a Call to Worship in the words of Holy Scripture. The invitation is from God. In response to this the people unite with the minister in a Prayer of Invocation seeking God's help in what they are about to do, or in a hymn of praise followed by Prayers of Approach—Adoration, Confession and Supplication. God speaks again in the lesson from the Old Testament and the congregation replies with an act of praise, or a cry for help to heed the Word of God, expressed in the words of a psalm or hymn. The proclamation of God's redeeming love in Jesus Christ in the reading of Epistle and Gospel again evokes praise, which may be followed by Intercession. The Ministry of the Word then comes to a burning focus in the sermon which relates the everlasting Gospel to present con-

[1] See J. R. P. Sclater, *The Public Worship of God,* pp. 25-26.

ditions and needs. Their minds and hearts kindled by this fresh vision, the congregation respond in the Offertory—the offering, not only of monetary gifts, but also of the sacramental bread and wine, the symbols of our toil and God's blessing, to be used as the channels of His grace—and in Intercession for all sorts and conditions of men, if this has not already been made. The service now moves to its climax in the dramatic symbolism of the Lord's Supper, setting forth as no words can the mystery of God's redeeming love in Jesus Christ. As *Sursum corda* (Lift up your hearts) is the key-note of the invitation to the Lord's Table, thanksgiving and self-oblation are the only proper response:

It is meet and right so to do.

'So worship develops with new unfoldings of the Divine character, which call forth new answers from men, who, all the while, are drawing nearer to God, and, thus, discovering more clearly the Heavenly Father's face.'[1]

The second movement within worship thus becomes clear. With the principle of alternation there is combined the principle of ascension.[2] The rhythm of call and answer, vision and response is not the movement of a pendulum but the progressive convolution of a spiral stair. As Sclater has pointed out, there is an almost unalterable ascending sequence of the emotions of man in his approach to God. Beginning with fear which then becomes awe, it changes to joy and finally to love. 'The fear of the Lord is the *beginning* of wisdom: and the end of the story is to know and to rest in the love that passeth knowledge. And, midway, fear blends with awe: and awe at God's majesty moves into

[1] Sclater, op. cit., p. 26.

[2] The nomenclature is Sclater's.

awe at His redeeming passion, whence springs joy that to ourselves is given new power and new life.'[1] It follows then that this sequence must find expression in the liturgical structure of a service if it is to be an effective vehicle of worship. 'Beginning with an attempt to see the Vision of God high and lifted up, we progress along an inevitable moment of consequent fear blending into awe, and thence to a new unveiling of the Divine nature, whence spring joy and love.'[2]

Translated into practical terms, this means that worship should begin on an objective note. The worshipper's attention must be focused upon God; not on his feelings about God; much less on his own needs. The first hymn should be a hymn setting forth the greatness, the majesty, the goodness, the holy love of God. If it is preceded by a Prayer of Invocation, this should be short. The Prayers of Approach following the hymn should begin with Adoration which leads naturally to Confession:

Woe is me! for I am undone; because I am a man of unclean lips, and I dwell in the midst of a people of unclean lips: for mine eyes have seen the King, the Lord of hosts (Isa. vi. 5).

After Confession and Absolution there follows Supplication for divine grace and strength. Thus ends the first stage of worship, the stage of Approach. Man, humble in the knowledge of his insufficiency and sin, bows in reverent awe before his Creator who is also his Redeemer, and awaits His Word of grace.

Clearly, Intercession, Thanksgiving and Oblation would be premature at this first stage of worship; they are evoked by the Ministry of the Word and should not normally

[1] ibid., p. 27. [2] ibid.

precede it. Only gradually is awe transformed into joy and love as the vision of Him who is of purer eyes than to behold iniquity becomes the vision of the Word made flesh, wounded for our transgressions and bruised for our iniquities, by whose stripes we are healed. We are brought back to the first basic liturgical principle: worship depends upon revelation; and Christian worship is the Church's response to the whole *biblical* revelation, beginning with the Call of Israel and culminating in the reconstitution of the People of God as the New Israel through the Birth and Ministry, Passion and Death, Resurrection and Exaltation of Jesus Christ. Hence in the central normative act of Christian worship the Ministry of the Word, read from the Old and New Testament Scriptures and proclaimed in the Sermon, should precede the main prayers of the service. There is one possible exception, however. It is permissible to put Intercession between the Gospel lection and the Sermon, thus bringing the needs of the Church and the world into intimate relationship with the Good News of Jesus Christ by inserting the Intercessions into the heart of the Ministry of the Word. This has been the traditional practice of Congregationalists, although it must be admitted that the preference of the early Independents for having the 'long' prayer before the Sermon seems to have been supported by inadequate liturgical reasons based upon 1 Tim. ii. 1. The more general Reformed practice has been to postpone Intercession until after the Sermon, and there is much to be said for it. As Marsh observes, 'Often the intercessions will come most appropriately after minds have been kindled, visions broadened, and sympathies stirred by the preaching of the Gospel.'[1]

[1] *A Book of Public Worship*, Introduction, p. xiv.

The main response of the worshippers belongs to the third stage of the service—the 'Liturgy of the Upper Room,' the Fellowship in prayer and sacrament which follows the Ministry of the Word. The transition is marked by the Offertory,[1] after which is the appropriate place for Intercession. A communion hymn may then be sung followed by the Words of Institution read as a warrant for observing the Lord's Supper. Then there may come an Exhortation or the 'Comfortable Words,' or the service may proceed straight to the great Consecration Prayer; Thanksgiving, Memorial of the Passion, and the Invocation of the Holy Spirit leading to Oblation followed by the saying together of the Lord's Prayer. After the Manual Acts (the breaking of the bread and lifting of the Cup)[2] and the reception of the elements, the service closes with a brief post-Communion Thanksgiving and prayer for a holy life, a hymn (before or during which an Offering for the poor may be received), and the dismissal of the congregation with the Blessing.

When there is no celebration of the Supper, Thanksgiving and Oblation precede, or follow, the Intercessions after the Offertory, and the prayers are gathered up by the saying together of the Lord's Prayer. If Intercession comes earlier in the service, as in the traditional Congregationalist practice, the Prayers of Thanksgiving and Oblation, followed by the Lord's Prayer, should be retained after the Sermon and Offertory as the climax of worship. In either case the Lord's Prayer is followed by a closing hymn and the Blessing. The custom of placing both Thanksgiving and Intercession before the Sermon, which has become very general in recent years, has the effect of assimilating the

[1] See pp. 159ff.

[2] See chapter VI, pp. 175-8.

structure of the eucharistic norm of worship to the structure of Anglican Morning Prayer, as the Sermon then comes at the end of the service. It may be argued, however, that the service is still, broadly speaking, eucharistic, since the Sermon is an integral part of it and not just 'tacked on' to an otherwise complete Office. Some would go further and maintain that the sacramental character of the service is assured by the very fact that it culminates in the 'sacrament' of the Preached Word. Be that is it may, the full eucharistic *structure* cannot be preserved unless the Liturgy of the Word is followed by at least some part of the Liturgy of the Upper Room.

A eucharistic service, whether it be a full celebration of the Lord's Supper or an Ante-Communion, should properly be conducted not from the pulpit but from the Communion Table, the focal centre of worship. In the Reformed tradition the minister leads the prayers of the congregation standing behind the Table facing the people (the 'basilican posture'). In a Methodist Church, where the Holy Table is placed altar-wise against the pulpit front or the East Wall (as in the Anglican tradition), he stands at the North end. The Lessons are read from the lectern and the minister proceeds to the pulpit during the hymn preceding the Sermon, returning to the Communion Table for the Offertory and the rest of the service. Where there is no lectern, the Lessons may be read from the pulpit, the minister remaining there until after the Sermon. In churches with a central pulpit placed immediately behind the Communion Table, the whole of the first part of the service may be conducted from the pulpit, but the minister should proceed to the Table to receive the Offerings and conduct the remainder of the service from there.

We have been concerned, so far, with the ordering of prayer in the morning service only. Since this is (or should be) the central act of Christian worship, the ideal is a weekly Eucharist in which Sermon and Sacrament take their proper place; where such is at present impracticable (as in the majority of Free Churches), the eucharistic structure should be preserved. If that is done, the other Sunday service should take the form of a Supplementary evening Office, for which the structure of Evensong or Compline is admirable. As Maxwell observes, 'By this means, useful variety would be obtained between morning and evening worship; and these beautiful Offices would not be lost to the Reformed Churches.'[1] Examples of evening orders of service, preserving the structure of the Quire Offices but in the Reformed tradition, may be found in *The Book of Common Order* of the Church of Scotland and *The Book of Common Worship* of the Presbyterian Church in the United States of America. Such a service may well begin with the traditional versicles and responses:

Minister: O Lord, open thou our lips.
People: And our mouth shall shew forth thy praise
Minister: O God, make speed to save us.
People: O Lord, make haste to help us.
Minister: Glory be to the Father, and to the Son, and to the Holy Ghost.
People: As it was in the beginning, is now, and ever shall be, world without end. Amen.
Minister: Praise ye the Lord.
People: The Lord's name be praised.

After an opening hymn, Prayers of Approach consisting of Invocation (or Adoration), Confession and Supplication are

[1] *An Outline of Christian Worship*, p. 170.

offered. Then a prose psalm is sung, or read responsively by minister and people (or a metrical psalm may be sung), followed by Lessons from the Old and New Testaments separated by a canticle or hymn. Prayers of Thanksgiving and Intercession with Commemoration of the Departed, concluding with the Lord's Prayer, may follow the New Testament Lesson, perhaps preceded (or divided) by an anthem or hymn. The Notices and Offertory with its Prayer of Oblation may fittingly come at this point. Then a hymn is sung and a Prayer for Illumination introduces the Sermon. Worship closes with another hymn, one or two evening Collects (e.g. from Compline), and the Blessing. The service may be conducted from the pulpit or from a prayer-desk (except for the Sermon), the minister proceeding to the Communion Table to receive and dedicate the Offerings and for the final prayers and Blessing.

IV SET FORMS AND FREE PRAYER

'If in transacting business,' says Calvin, 'some form must always be observed, which public decency and therefore humanity itself require us not to disregard, this ought specially to be observed in churches.' Worship requires forms because it is a corporate activity, corporate acts by their very nature setting restrictions to individual freedom. If people are to sing or play or dance *together,* there must be some agreed procedure in which they all participate; unrestricted individual freedom can only result in chaos. 'The common mind of a society requires a formula to express its common thought.'[1] This is true of all corporate worship, even that of the most individualistic type such as a meeting

[1] J. E. Rattenbury, *Vital Elements of Public Worship*, p. 12.

of the Society of Friends. The fact that the Friends meet in a certain place at a particular time and observe an agreed procedure, namely silence, is itself a 'form' by which their worship is expressed. In the last analysis therefore, the question is not whether there shall be forms or no forms, but of what kind the forms shall be.

The expression of public prayer can only be profitably discussed against this general background. The antithesis of liturgical *versus* free prayer is not one of form *versus* no-form; the most spontaneous extemporary prayer is no less a form than is a classic litany. The issue is that of good forms or bad. The inescapable question for Free Churchmen, whose liturgical freedom has been so dearly bought, is therefore: What forms are most adequate for the expression of this vital response of the worshipping Church—corporate prayer?

Two prelimnary considerations must be noted at this stage. First, the Puritan tradition in which Baptists, Congregationalists and Presbyterians stand does not, when considered as a whole, commit its heirs to any one particular form of prayer. Within Puritanism itself we find a variety of liturgical emphases, ranging from a radical repudiation of all set forms, including the Lord's Prayer, to the attempt in 1584 to substitute 'A Booke of the Forme of Common Prayers' for the Anglican Prayer Book as the uniform liturgy of the land.[1] The moderate Puritans were not opposed to a liturgy in principle but only to a particular liturgy, the Book of Common Prayer; they objected, not to liturgical forms as such, but to the 'stinted forms' of the Prayer Book. This

[1] See Bancroft, *Dangerous Positions* (1595), III. x. 96f, and Hooker, *Eccl. Pol.,* V. xxvii. 1. This book is known as the Waldegrave Liturgy.

is clearly evident from the existence of Knox's Genevan Service Book (1556), the Waldegrave Liturgy (1584), the Middleburgh Liturgy (1586), the Westminster Directory (1644) and Baxter's Savoy Liturgy (1661). On the other hand, even the Presbyterians, who inclined most strongly toward a prescribed form of prayer, insisted that the liturgy must not exclude the exercise of the gift of extemporary prayer.[1] The provision in the Westminster Directory of 1644 for both liturgical and free prayer is sufficient evidence of the comprehensiveness of the Puritan tradition.

Second, the liturgical liberty of which Free Churchmen rightly boast is a positive and not just a negative freedom. It is not merely freedom from the manacles of the Book of Common Prayer, nor is it only liberty to exercise the gift of extemporary prayer; it is also freedom to make use of whatever we are led to appropriate from the rich liturgical heritage of the whole Church. We may, if we will, select freely, under the guidance of the Holy Spirit, from all the liturgical traditions of Christendom. All things are ours.

The two classic modes of worship now claim our attention. We shall look at them briefly and attempt to assess the respective merits and defects of liturgical and free prayer.

1. *Liturgical Prayer.* One of the most obvious advantages of a liturgy is that it saves the congregation from being at the mercy of the minister's moods. The content of the prayers and the balance of the service are unaffected by the disposition or temper of the one who conducts it. Worship thus gains in objectivity and stability. Dignity and orderliness are also ensured. So is catholicity: a traditional

[1] 'Exceptions against the Book of Common Prayer' presented to the Bishops at the Savoy Conference, 1661. See Bayne, *Puritan Documents,* p. 114f.

liturgy unites the worshipping congregation with believers of past days; it enshrines the experience of many generations of Christians, embodying as it does 'the accumulated wisdom and beauty of the Christian Church, the garnered excellence of the saints.'[1] Furthermore, a classic Collect, for instance, 'combines the collective and the individual, in a way in which perhaps only long usage can do.'[2] Another outstanding merit of the ancient liturgies, too often overlooked by Free Churchmen, is emphasized in the Faith and Order Commission's Report, *Ways of Worship:* 'The traditional forms of liturgy are throughout scriptural, both in their spirit and in their choice of language.'[3] Again, a classic liturgy, as F. H. Brabant points out, has an impressive or suggestive function: it 'not only expresses what we feel; it also teaches us what we ought to feel.'[4]

The defects of a set form of prayers are equally obvious. If everything is rigidly prescribed, what room is there for the spontaneous promptings of the Holy Spirit? This is the real ground of the Puritans' objection to the imposition of an inflexible liturgy. Appealing to Rom. viii. 26: 'Likewise the Spirit also helpeth our infirmities; for we know not what we should pray for as we ought; but the Spirit itself maketh intercession for us with groanings which cannot be uttered,' they maintain that bondage to set forms means the virtual quenching of the Spirit.[5] Minister and people are thus deprived of the Spirit-given gift of prayer. 'We cannot

1 P. Dearmer, quoted by K. L. Parry, 'Prayer and Praise' in *Christian Worship* (ed. N. Micklem), p. 234.

2 K. L. Parry, op. cit., p. 234.

3 p. 18, section A.

4 'Worship in General' in *Liturgy and Worship* (ed. Clarke and Harris), p. 13.

5 See John Owen, *A Discourse of the Work of the Holy Spirit in Prayer; Works* (ed. Russell), iv. 92.

believe,' say the ejected ministers of 1662, 'that it is lawful for us at all times, by submitting ourselves to a Form of Prayer, to smother the Gift of Prayer, given (we hope) to some of us, or to cool the heat and fervency of our hearts in Prayer, or the Affections of them that hear us.'[1] Again, a set form, comprehensive and catholic though it be, lacks particularity; it is unrelated to the varying needs of different people and times. For this reason Isaac Watts, who admits the value of set forms, refuses to be confined to a prescribed form of prayer:

> For it is not possible that forms of prayer should be composed, that are perfectly suited to all our occasions in the things of this life and the life to come. Our circumstances are always altering in this frail and mutable state. We have new sins to be confessed, new temptations and sorrows to be represented, new wants to be supplied. Every change of providence in the affairs of a nation, a family, or a person, requires suitable petitions and acknowledgements. And all these can never be well provided for in any prescribed composition.[2]

Another defect of a liturgy is that it tends to become stale through much repetition and hence may conduce to hypocrisy, the worshippers expressing what they do not really feel.[3]

2. *Free Prayer* avoids these particular pitfalls. It has the advantage of spontaneity; the minister has full liberty to respond to the promptings of the Spirit as he feels led to

1 *A Sober and Temperate Discourse concerning the Interest of Words in Prayer* by H.D.M.A. (London 1661), p. 96. Cf John Owen, *A Discourse concerning Liturgies and their Imposition* (1662), *Works* (ed. Goold, Edinburgh 1862), xv. 52.

2 *Guide to Prayer; Works,* iv. 127.

3 See Isaac Watts, ibid.

give them utterance. Springing as it does (or should do) from an intimate pastoral relationship of minister and people, it is related to the worshippers' particular conditions and needs. 'In a memorable phrase, Owen refers to "a recoiling of efficacy" resulting from the extemporary prayers of ministers who have thought devoutly on the grace and majesty of God and of the needs of their congregations.'[1] Again, free prayer enables the minister to gather up and express the feelings of his people on those rare occasions when he is able to sense them intuitively at some particular stage of the service. It thus links the congregation with the free charismatic worship of the Apostolic Church.

But free prayer too has grave defects. Ministers, being human, have their moods; and it is fatally easy for the minister, without realizing that he is doing it, to inflict his own state of mind upon a congregation through his prayers. At best, this may result in a lack of objectivity in the service; at worst, it may entirely vitiate worship. Free prayer may also deprive worship of objectivity by being excessively didactic. Ostensibly it is offered to God; actually it may be addresed to the congregation. It may be more concerned with edification than with adoration. Another potential defect is lack of dignity and order. Hooker, castigating the Puritans, complains of 'the irksome deformities whereby, through endless and senseless effusions of indigested Prayers, they oftentimes disgrace in most insufferable manner the worthiest part of Christian duty towards God, who herein are subject to no certain order, but pray both what and how they list.'[2] A caricature maybe, but like all caricatures having

[1] Horton Davies, *The Worship of the English Puritans,* p. 106. The reference is to *A Discourse of the Work of the Holy Spirit in Prayer; Works* (ed. Russell), iv. 92.

[2] *Eccl. Pol.,* V. xxv. 5.

a basis in fact. The note of catholicity also may be missing in free prayer, though it need not be. But the very fact of its preoccupation with local conditions and present needs may result in its being unrelated to the wider witness and past life of the Church. Jeremy Taylor puts his finger upon two further defects, one relating to the minister and the other to the congregation. He charges ministers with making a pretence of the Spirit a cover for mental laziness and asks, 'Whether it is better to pray to God with consideration, or without? Whether is the wiser man of the two, he who thinks, and deliberates what to say, or he that utters his mind as fast as it comes?'[1] Congregations, he maintains, are hindered in their devotion, 'for they dare not say *Amen* till they have considered; and many such cases will occur in *ex tempore* prayers that need much considering before we can attest them.[2] Finally, it is not unknown for free prayer to be free in name only but virtually fixed in form and 'so far as content is concerned, even more formal than the common liturgical ritual.'[3] Without due thought and careful preparation it tends, all too often, to petrify into stereotyped phrases and *clichés;* so acquiring the defects of a set form without necessarily possessing the scriptural character of the traditional liturgies.

Clearly no one mode of public prayer is adequate in itself, a fact to which the protagonists of the sixteenth and seventeenth centuries seem, for the most part, to have been curiously blind. 'If the Anglican missed the spontaneity, simplicity, intimacy and purity of free prayer, the Puritan

[1] *Two Discourses* (London 1682), p. 1.

[2] Quoted by Horton Davies, op. cit., p. 109.

[3] J. H. Miller, *The Practice of Public Prayer,* quoted by J. E. Rattenbury, op. cit., p. 81.

equally overlooked the uniformity, dignity, catholicity and order of the Book of Common Prayer.'[1] Each has its merits; neither is free from defects. Moreover, as Horton Davies points out, 'the two different types of prayer, liturgical and free, appear to reflect . . . two differing conceptions of the Church. The former stresses the corporate nature of the Church in "Common Prayer," the latter emphasizes the need of individuals in a family Church. If liturgical prayer adequately reflects what is held in common in its Creeds, its General Confession, its abstract Collects praying for graces required by all Christians, then free prayer meets the individual's particular requirements.'[2] What at least the more extreme members of each camp seemed to have failed to realize is that they are not mutually exclusive. The one is the complement of the other and corporate prayer is best expressed by a judicious blending of both. As the Faith and Order Commission remarks, 'The practical problem is that of deciding the appropriate place for each.'[3]

Much depends upon the type of church envisaged. While it is true that 'the differing conceptions of worship derive . . . to a considerable extent from differing ecclesiologies,'[4] the two conceptions of the Church implied are not incompatible but complementary; but the emphasis will vary in different places. Where a church serves a large community there is need for a formal liturgical service in which free prayer has a relatively small place; in a more closely-knit fellowship, where there is an intimate pastoral relationship

[1] Horton Davies, op. cit., p. 110.

[2] ibid., p. 105.

[3] *Ways of Worship*, p. 28.

[4] Horton Davies, op. cit., p. 105.

between minister and people, worship may well be less liturgical and free prayer have a larger place.[1]

Free prayer does not necessarily mean extemporary prayer, which is spontaneous and unpremeditated, springing directly out of the occasion (*ex tempore*). It may equally well mean what Isaac Watts calls 'conceived prayer,' that is, prayer which is carefully prepared by the minister in advance. If not actually written down beforehand, the contents and sequence of such prayer will be clearly worked out in the minister's mind. This is the kind of free prayer advocated by Matthew Henry and Isaac Watts who are as critical of the abuses of extemporary prayer as Jeremy Taylor and Hooker. Matthew Henry maintains that

> it is requisite to the decent Performance of the Duty, that some proper Method be observ'd, not only that what is said be good, but that it be said in its proper Place and Time; and that we offer not any thing to the Glorious Majesty of Heaven and Earth, which is confus'd, impertinent, and indigested.[2]

Similarly, Isaac Watts, in his classic *Guide to Prayer* (1716), warns against 'an entire dependence on sudden motions and suggestions of thought.'[3] As a general rule, free prayer in

[1] This principle underlies John Wesley's practice. 'Notwithstanding his belief in extemporary prayer, providing it was short, Wesley believed that the *normal* worship of the people would be better expressed by Liturgical forms.' For Wesley *normal* worship meant *parish* worship. In the more intimate circle of the Methodist society extemporary prayer was used but this presupposed, for Wesley, the background of the liturgy of the Parish Church. The devotional exercises of his societies were meant to be *supplementary* to parish worship. For his Travelling Preachers in America, where no such background existed, Wesley prepared in 1784 'a Liturgy differing little from that of the Church of England to use on the Lord's Day in all the congregations.' See Rattenbury, op. cit., pp. 80-81.

[2] *A Method of Prayer* (London 1710), p. A4 *recto*.

[3] *Works,* iv. 125.

worship should be 'conceived' rather than 'extemporary.' If a man is lifted out of himself in a moment of inspiration, by all means let him put aside what he has prepared and follow the leading of the Spirit: the wind bloweth where it listeth. But not to every man is given this gift of impromptu prayer; neither is it of frequent occurrence. To count upon the earthquake, wind and fire in the pulpit may be to miss the still small voice in the study. The minister who knows what he is about spends many hours, not to say days, in careful preparation of the word that he is to speak on God's behalf to his people: should he be any less diligent in preparing what he is commissioned to say on the people's behalf to God?

Let John Oman speak the final word: 'I have often been puzzled,' he says, 'about what makes a service worship. It does not depend either upon having a liturgy or wanting it. It does not depend on the sincerity or even the piety of the minister. More and more I come to think that it depends on worshipping with the congregation, and not merely conducting their worship.'[1]

[1] *Office of the Ministry*, p. 11.

CHAPTER V

Church Praise

I MUSIC AND WORSHIP

NEARLY sixteen hundred years ago a memorable baptismal service was held in the cathedral at Milan. One of those baptized was an ex-professor of rhetoric—St. Augustine. Significantly enough, the feature of that service which he particularly recalls is the intense emotional impression made upon both himself and the congregation by the singing of hymns—a practice recently introduced by St. Ambrose the bishop.[1]

St. Augustine's experience on that day has been the experience of Christian men and women through the centuries. With him they have found that as tones flowed into their ears the truth distilled in their heart. What Keats calls 'music's golden tongue' has spoken to them of the unutterably deep things of God. 'Words speak to our thoughts,' says Kingsley, 'but music speaks to our heart and spirit, to the very core and root of our souls.'

Music, as 'the handmaid of religion,' has a two-fold place in public worship. First, church music of the right kind may serve an important, if subsidiary, purpose as an aid to worship. F. H. Brabant observes that 'if we all arrived (at church) feeling and thinking as we ought, no doubt our services would be simply the expression in speech and action of the inner state of our souls with all the spontaneous directness of children. But we do not, most of us,

[1] *Confessions,* IX, 7.

arrive like that. We come, stained and weary from a life that is largely unnatural, longing for something to lift us up into an atmosphere of spiritual peace.' Hence, worship 'has not only an expressive function but also a suggestive or impressive one.'[1] Brabant is speaking with special reference to the impressive use of the liturgy as not only expressing what the worshipper feels but also suggesting to him what he ought to feel. But what he says is applicable in a broader sense to all church art. Gothic architecture, diffused light, stained glass, all combine to make us suggestible to the things of the Spirit; they dispose the mind to worship. The same is true of church music; the tones of instrument and voice, no less than the frozen music of the Gothic arch, can lead men into the secret place of the Most High.

If it is true that the sight of York Minster or Westminster Abbey or any beautiful church can dispose ordinary men's minds to worship as they sit in the nave and look around, and surrender themselves to all the signs of beauty that surround them, no less surely the sound of the Hallelujah Chorus or the 'St. Anne' fugue or any beautiful anthem can do the very same thing, perhaps even more movingly. If it is true that an east window, full of light and depicting suggestions of the story of Christendom, can help men, women and children to concentrate upon the story and realize it more vividly, so can Bach's Passion Music or Elgar's 'Apostles.' The worshipper has no personal part to play in the beautiful thing seen or heard, except to receive, see or hear in reverence what is offered in reverent aid.[2]

Hence the high calling of church musicians. To the organist and choir there is entrusted the responsibility of providing the medium of music through which the spiritual

[1] *Liturgy and Worship*, p. 13.

[2] Walford Davies and Harvey Grace, *Music and Worship*, p. 24.

world is brought near. Their contribution is as real as is the chancel arch and the east window. They must labour to perfect it with no less diligence than the architect, the artist and the sculptor. They must seek to convey through the 'Beauty of Wholeness' the reality of the Beauty of Holiness.

There is a subtle danger which besets church musicians; not the slack and careless ones, but the most thorough and painstaking. It is the danger of making the music of worship an end in itself, instead of a means to a greater end. Thus the very thing which should lead men into the presence of God may become a vain show which distracts their minds from Him. That which should point them to the ultimate Truth allures them to itself and veils from their eyes the Reality by which men live. Few men have been more aware of this danger than was St. Augustine. In a moving passage in his *Confessions* he speaks of the allurements of the pleasures of the ear and the temptation to give music an undue place.

Yet there are times when through too great a fear of this temptation, I err in the direction of over-severity—even to the point sometimes of wishing that the melody of all the lovely airs with which David's Psalter is commonly sung should be banished not only from my own ears, but from the Church's as well : and that seems to me a safer course. . . . Yet when I remember the tears I shed, moved by the songs of the Church in the early days of my new faith : and again when I see that I am moved not by the singing but by the things that are sung—when they are sung with a clear voice and proper modulation—I recognise once more the usefulness of this practice. Thus I fluctuate between the peril of indulgence and the profit I have found : and on the whole I am inclined . . . to approve the custom of singing in Church, that by the pleasure of the ear the weaker minds may be roused to a feeling of devotion. Yet whenever it happens that I am more moved by the singing than by the thing that is sung, I admit that I have grievously sinned, and then I should wish rather not to have heard the singing.[1]

This was the ground of the puritan objection which banished from the Calvinistic Churches of Holland all symbolism and ornament, and put an end to the music of organ and choir. As J. S. Whale points out,[2] 'it did not necessarily mean distrust of beauty and the arts for their own sake'; and, in fact, the apparent austerity of sixteenth century Calvinistic worship was mitigated to a large extent by the congregational singing which Luther and Calvin restored. The truth is that the excesses of the Roman Mass had made men afraid lest the magic of beauty should become a snare.

Should we then banish beauty and the arts from worship? God forbid! All good things may be abused and *corruptio optimi pessima,* the corruption of the best becomes the worst. But, as Luther was wise enough to insist, *abusus non tollit usum*—abuse does not invalidate use. The danger will be avoided if the true end of worship is upheld—the setting forth of the majesty, the glory, and the grace of God. The Puritans were by no means lacking in good taste, as A. L. Drummond has shown;[3] if they worshipped in barns and warehouses, it was, as K. L. Parry points out, of necessity and not of choice.[4] It was a Puritan who wrote:

> But let my due feet never fail
> To walk the studious cloisters pale,
> And love the high embowèd roof,
> With antic pillars massy proof,
> And storied windows richly dight,

[1] X. 33 (F. J. Sheed's translation).

[2] See 'Calvin' in *Christian Worship* (ed. N. Micklem), pp. 161-5.

[3] See *The Church Architecture of Protestantism,* pp. 43-45.

[4] 'Prayer and Praise' in *Christian Worship* (ed. N. Micklem), p. 237.

Casting a dim religious light.
There let the pealing organ blow,
To the full-voiced quire below,
In service high and anthem clear,
As may with sweetness, through mine ear,
Dissolve me into ecstacies,
And bring all heaven before mine eyes.[1]

Secondly, in addition to this impressive or suggestive function, church music has also an expressive function. Not only is in an aid to worship; it is also, as Walford Davies and Harvey Grace rightly insist, a means of worship. 'If song were not at least as natural and spontaneous a human act as speech, there would be no question of music becoming an actual carrier of public worship itself. It could still be an aid, perhaps. . . . But men could never have sung the very words of their worship together.'[2] Art, as they point out, is not opposed to nature. When a child is too happy to walk, it begins, quite spontaneously, to dance. Similarly, speech when charged with emotion may become song, as in the *hwyl* of impassioned Welsh preachers. Then, 'Is not musical utterance, at moments, indeed the very best vehicle of public worship, just as spoken utterance is at other moments?' Indeed 'melodic utterance of a simple and wholly fitting order can become as natural to a normal Christian assembly as corporate speech, and far more beautiful.'[3] But when people dance or sing together, spontaneity must be organized, it must find expression in certain forms. Since then worship is essentially corporate, the spontaneous outburst of praise must be expressed in a way in which all

[1] John Milton, *Il Penseroso.*

[2] See op. cit., pp. 44f.

[3] ibid., pp. 61-62.

can join harmoniously. Failure to grasp this simple principle caused confusion in the Corinthian Church. 'When ye come together,' says St. Paul, 'every one of you hath a psalm, hath a doctrine, hath a tongue, hath a revelation, hath an interpretation. Let all things be done unto edifying. . . . For God is not the author of confusion, but of peace.'[1]

II PSALMS AND HYMNS

The forms through which corporate praise finds expression are the psalm and the hymn. The Christian Church inherited congregational singing from the Jewish Synagogue and its first hymn-book was the Psalter. In these songs of Zion Christians found fitting vehicles of their praise; the psalms that they had sung in the synagogue took on a new meaning for them because in Jesus Christ God had visited and redeemed His people. When they sang, 'The Lord is my shepherd; I shall not want,' they thought of the Good Shepherd who had given his life for the sheep. Psalm ii spoke to them of the commissioning of Christ, Psalm xxii of His Passion, and Psalm xxiv of His Exaltation and glory.

For over nineteen centuries the Hebrew psalms have formed the basis of Christian praise. As we have seen, the daily worship of the medieval Church was built around the orderly singing or recitation of the whole Psalter once a week. The psalms provided the Introit at the beginning of the Mass, the Gradual sung on the altar step (*gradus*) between the Epistle and the Gospel, and the Offertory and Communion praise. The congregational singing for which the Reformed worship at Geneva became noted was limited to the metrical psalm, *la sirène calviniste,* as the Lutherans

[1] 1 Cor. xiv. 26-33.

enviously described it.[1] Indeed, for a century and a half the metrical psalm remained the only form of congregational praise in the Reformed Churches. The psalm has therefore a unique place as the classic form of praise, and we may not dispense with it without cutting ourselves off from historic liturgical tradition and radically altering the character of Christian worship.

The Christian Psalter . . . brings to the worshipper's heart and lips the perfect devotional life of Jesus, who lived and died by it. Furthermore, it joins him to the vast company in heaven . . . and on earth who day by day, week by week, month by month, year by year, have striven to form their lives on Jesus' life, and to praise the Father as he did in his holy Manhood on earth. Do we . . . suggest that the Psalter is an outmoded encumbrance, to be perfunctorily dealt with, until we gain sufficient iconoclastic courage to abandon it, and substitute a Gospel hymn? If so, we strike at the very life of all sound Church music, because we cut off the main stream of Christian praise.[2]

At least one psalm, either in prose or metre, should have a place in every full act of Christian worship. In a service of eucharistic structure the traditional place of a psalm would be either at the beginning as the opening act of praise (the Introit of the Mass), or between the Scripture Lessons (the Gradual of the Mass), or at the Offertory (the Offertory Psalm of the Mass), or during the delivery and reception of the elements (the Communion Chant of the Mass). Suitable metrical psalms may be used equally well at any, or all, of these places in the service (although silence may be preferred during the communion of the people), but a

[1] See J. S. Whale, *Christian Worship,* p. 164.

[2] W. Douglas, *Church Music in History and Practice,* pp. 135-6.

prose psalm is most appropriately chanted between the Lessons. So used, it makes a fitting link between the readings of the Old and New Testaments, or the Epistle and the Gospel, as a part of the Ministry of the Word. The purpose of the *Gloria Patri,*[1] with which a prose psalm should always conclude, is to turn a Jewish psalm into a Christian act of praise 'by affirming belief in the God who, though only fully revealed in Trinity to the Church of the New Testament, is nevertheless truly known by the Church of the Old.'[2] In a service having the structure of a Quire Office, the psalm (or psalms) forms an act of praise immediately following the versicles and responses (as in Anglican Morning and Evening Prayer) or the Prayers of Approach (as in Reformed services of Office structure), and *before* the Scripture Lessons.

The psalms are meant to be sung, not said; and they should be sung, either in prose or in metre, whenever possible. Furthermore, the metrical psalm, however dignified and beautiful, can never be an *entirely* satisfactory substitute for the chanted prose psalm, preserving at it does the actual phrases and rhythms of Scripture. The metrical psalm should by all means be retained, not only on account of its intrinsic beauty, but also because it forms an unbroken link with early Reformed worship; but the chanting of prose psalms also needs to be revived from the disuse into which it has fallen in many Free Churches. Modern speech-rhythm is not beyond the powers of even a congregation of very average musical ability, provided it is led by a well-trained

1 Glory be to the Father, and to the Son, and to the Holy Ghost; As it was in the beginning, is now, and ever shall be, world without end. Amen.

2 E. C. Ratcliff, 'The Choir Offices,' *Liturgy and Worship,* p. 272.

choir; and the single or double 'Anglican' chant, majestic in its simplicity, stands unrivalled as a form of praise. Needless to say, chanting should never be hurried; it is not meant to be executed in strict time but after the manner of recitative, with due regard to the phrasing and punctuation of the psalm. When it is not possible to sing the psalms, they may be read responsively by minister and people, the minister reading as far as the caesura (or colon) and the congregation the rest of the verse. This is preferable to the reading of alternate verses, since Hebrew poetry consists of couplets, the second part of each completing, or contrasting with, the first. Psalm xxiv provides a typical example:

Minister: The earth is the Lord's, and the fulness thereof;
People: The world, and they that dwelt therein.
Minister: For he hath founded it upon the seas,
People: And established it upon the floods.
Minister: Who shall ascend into the hill of the Lord?
People: Or who shall stand in his holy place?
Minister: He that hath clean hands and a pure heart;
People: Who hath not lifted up his soul unto vanity, nor sworn deceitfully.
Minister: He shall receive the blessing from the Lord,
People: And righteousness from the God of his salvation.
Minister: This is the generation of them that seek him,
People: That seek thy face, O Jacob.
Minister: Lift up your heads, O ye gates; and be ye lift up, ye everlasting doors;
People: And the King of glory shall come in.
Minister: Who is this King of glory?
People: The Lord strong and mighty, the Lord mighty in battle.

Minister: Lift up your heads, O ye gates; even lift them up, ye everlasting doors;

People: And the King of glory shall come in.

Minister: Who is this King of glory?

People: The Lord of hosts, he is the King of glory.

Minister:[1] Glory be to the Father, and to the Son, and to the Holy Ghost;

People: As it was in the beginning, is now, and ever shall be, world without end. Amen.

A psalm read responsively, as we have previously noted,[2] should not be confused with the Scripture lections; it is a corporate act of praise and not a substitute for the Old Testament Lesson.

Although the Early Church made full use of the Jewish Psalter, it did not limit its praise entirely to the psalms. Christians themselves composed hymns on Christian themes. We find fragments of these in various parts of the New Testament. St. Paul, in his Letter to the Ephesians, quotes some lines of one:

Awake thou that sleepest,
And arise from the dead,
And Christ shall give thee light (Eph. v. 14).

An extract from another appears in the First Epistle to Timothy:

God was manifest in the flesh, justified in the Spirit,
Seen of angels, preached unto the Gentiles,
Believed on in the world, received up into glory.
(1 Tim. ii. 16).

We find yet another in the Second Epistle to Timothy:

[1] The whole *Gloria Patri* may be said by minister and people in unison.

[2] Chapter iii, p. 48.

For if we be dead with him, we shall also live with him :
If we suffer, we shall also reign with him :
If we deny him, he also will deny us :
If we believe not, yet he abideth faithful.

(2 Tim. ii. 11-13).

Sometimes other portions of Scripture beside the psalms were sung. One such was the Song of Moses in Exodus xv:

The Lord is my strength and song, and he is become my salvation :
He is my God, and I will prepare him an habitation;
My father's God, and I will exalt him.

Three others were taken from St. Luke's Gospel—the songs of Zacharias, Mary and Simeon, which we know respectively (from their opening words in the Latin Vulgate) as the Benedictus, the Magnificat, and the Nunc Dimittis. New compositions in the style of these soon appeared, three of which—coming from very early times—still survive. The English version of one is sung at the end of the Anglican and Methodist Communion Services. It begins, 'Glory be to God on high, and in earth peace, good will towards men,' and was originally a morning hymn intended to be sung at dawn. Along with it was an evening hymn, for use at dusk as the church lamps were being lit, and translated into English by Keble in 1834, as, 'Hail, gladdening Light.' The third is the *Te Deum,* belonging to the fourth century and generally considered to be the work of Niceta the bishop of Remesiana. It is at the end of this same century that St. Ambrose, bishop of Milan, appears as the real pioneer of Christian hymns. His introduction of them was a novelty at the cathedral of Milan, which soon became noted for its impressive congregational praise.

The singing of both psalms and hymns belongs properly to the congregation; they are the vehicles of the people's praise. But in the Dark Ages congregational singing was lost. The medieval hymn was sung only by the clergy who formed the choir and hence it became more elaborate in form and structure. This, as F. C. Burkitt points out,[1] was the origin of the modern anthem which was retained as a hymn for the choir after the Reformation had restored congregational singing to its rightful place. The contributions of Luther and Calvin have already been noted. While Calvin limited the people's praise to the metrical psalm, Luther composed hymns of his own, *Ein' feste Burg ist unser Gott,* translated by Thomas Carlyle as 'A safe stronghold our God is still,' being a notable example. In England the metrical psalms of Sternhold and Hopkins held the field until the beginning of the eighteenth century when Isaac Watts revolutionized church praise.

He was the creator of the modern English hymn; which is neither an Office Hymn like Wither's or Ken's or Austin's, nor yet a metrical psalm, nor again a close paraphrase of Scripture, but a new species, evolved from the last named, and acquiring in the process a novel liberty of treatment and a balanced artistic form.[2]

The title of Watts's book, *The Psalms of David imitated in New Testament Language together with Hymns and Spiritual Songs,* is self-explanatory. B. L. Manning's concise description of its contents may be quoted:

It has two parts, as the title indicates, and they are of about equal length. In the first part Dr. Watts presents a metrical version of the Book of Psalms. It is not a mere reproduction of the 150 psalms. Some are omitted. Some are abbreviated. Some are represented by more than one version in different metres.

[1] *Christian Worship,* p. 105.

[2] Frere's 'Introduction' in the Historical Edition of *Hymns Ancient and Modern,* p. lxxxiii.

Some are divided into several parts. All are baptized into the Christian faith. . . .

The second part of the book contains hymns. First comes a book of hymns 'collected from the Holy Scriptures'—that is to say, paraphrases of both Old and New Testament passages. Second is a book of hymns 'composed on Divine Subjects'—that is to say, hymns as we should understand the word, freely composed without particular reference to Holy Scripture. Third, and last, are hymns 'prepared for the holy ordinance of the Lord's Supper.' As Watts had ended his Psalter by six versions of *Gloria Patri* in various metres, so he ends the hymn-book by others. Some are in the form of hymns. Some are single verses. To these he adds four hosannas to the Son of God. The result is a very substantial volume.[1]

Isaac Watts expresses his great aim, in departing from the literalism of current versions of the psalms, as being 'to teach my author to speak like a Christian.'[2] He succeeded, however, not only in christianizing the Psalter but also in establishing the hymn in English worship. By so doing 'he restored Christian praise to its rightful place in the Dissenting worship of the early eighteenth century'[3] and so revived the dying devotion of the age.

The Puritan tradition of hymnody which flowered in Isaac Watts was supplemented and enriched by the Evangelical tradition stemming from John and Charles Wesley. As B. L. Manning observes, 'No one can read Watts without having Wesley in mind, and nothing will enable a man to see the greatness of Watts's hymns so well as a thorough knowledge of Wesley's.'[4] Watts published his *Hymns* in 1707[5] and the

[1] *The Hymns of Wesley and Watts,* pp. 80-81.

[2] *Works,* iv. 119.

[3] Horton Davies, op. cit., p. 178.

[4] op. cit., p. 78.

[5] A second enlarged edition appeared in 1709.

Psalms in 1719; alongside of them must therefore be placed *A Collection of Hymns for the Use of the People called Methodists* by John Wesley, which appeared in 1780. This book, says Manning, 'ranks in Christian literature with the Psalms, the Book of Common Prayer, the Canon of the Mass.'[1] Wesley himself describes it as 'a little body of experimental and practical divinity.' 'Experimental' religion did not mean, for Wesley, subjectivism; it meant the personal appropriation of the historic faith. 'Wesley's confidence is rooted in the orthodox, catholic, evangelical faith. . . . Nothing is more untrue than to represent the heart of Wesley's religion as personal experience or even personal feeling. The heart of Wesley's religion is sound doctrine.'[2] Manning sums up the distinctive qualities of Wesley's hymns under three heads. First, their dogmatic content; they are a full-orbed contemplation of the catholic, evangelical faith of Christendom. Second, their empirical nature; they tell of a living experience of that faith:

> What we have felt and seen
> With confidence we tell.

And third, their mystical quality; they reflect the 'divine audacity' of one who has sat in heavenly places with Christ.

> There is the solid structure of historic dogma; there is the passionate thrill of present experience; but there is, too, the glory of a mystic sunlight coming directly from another world. This transfigures history and experience. This puts past and present into the timeless eternal NOW. . . . It is Wesley's glory that he united these three strains—dogma, experience, mysticism—in verse so simple that it could be understood, and so smooth that it could be used, by plain men.[3]

[1] op. cit., p. 14.

[2] B. L. Manning, op. cit., pp. 74-75.

[3] ibid., pp. 27-30.

The Church today has thus a three-fold heritage of hymnody: it inherits the Catholic tradition of St. Ambrose and the Middle Ages, reinforced by the Tractarians—Faber, Keble and Newman; it is the heir to the Puritan tradition of Milton and Doddridge, exemplified supremely in Isaac Watts; and to it is bequeathed the Evangelical tradition of Zinzendorf and the Moravians which flowers so finely in John and Charles Wesley.

III USES OF HYMNS

There is a radical difference between the use of hymns in Anglican worship and their function in a Free Church service. In the ordered worship of the Church of England hymns are extra-liturgical; they do not form a part of the actual liturgy but precede or follow it, as did their predecessors, the metrical psalms of the sixteenth and seventeenth centuries. The liturgy—whether it be the Eucharistic Office or Morning or Evening Prayer—is complete in itself quite apart from them.

The charter of hymn-singing in the Church of England is the 49th of the Royal Injunctions of Queen Elizabeth (1559), in which it was permitted 'for the comforting of such that delight in music . . . that in the beginning, or in the end of Common Prayers, either at morning or evening, there may be sung an hymn, or such-like song, to the praise of Almighty God, in the best sort of melody and music that may be conveniently devised.'[1]

The hymns referred to were, of course, metrical psalms, which were quite independent of the prose psalms for the

[1] F. C. Burkitt, *Christian Worship*, pp. 109-10.

day recited in the actual Office. In Free Church worship, however, hymns, far from being extra-liturgical, are an integral and indeed vital part of the service itself;[1] they form its permanent liturgical framework. Hence they discharge the functions of various constituent parts of a liturgy.[2] Whereas in the Anglican tradition their use is normally limited to supplying the opening and closing praise of worship (although outside the Office proper),[3] in Free Church services they may also voice the corporate prayer of the congregation and express their confession of faith.

1. *An Act of Praise*. The chief function of a hymn is to be the expression of the Church's praise. If Christian worship is the response of the Christian Church to the Christian revelation, praise must be its characteristic note. It is indeed of the very essence of all true worship: we assemble and meet together 'to set forth his most worthy praise.'

Both the impressive and the expressive functions of worship reach their culmination in praise. For in praise we express with heart and mind and soul the excellence and glory of God. 'Let all that is within me bless his holy name.' In praise, too, we set forth the majesty and love of God. 'I will give thee thanks in the great congregation.' Praise is also the way of communion with God. 'Let us come before his presence with thanksgiving . . .' Moreover, the very act of praise implies a

[1] Cf. K. L. Parry, 'Prayer and Praise' in *Christian Worship* (ed. N. Micklem), p. 240: 'After extempore prayer the Congregational hymn is the most characteristic feature of Free Church worship.'

[2] See B. L. Manning, op. cit., p. 133: 'Hymns are for us Dissenters what the liturgy is for the Anglican. They are the framework, the setting, the conventional, the traditional part of divine service as we use it. They are, to adopt the language of the liturgiologists, the Dissenting Use.'

[3] The exception is an 'Office Hymn.' See C. S. Phillips, op. cit., pp. 97-98.

conception of God. It is the most characteristic Christian act of worship.[1]

The two elements in the worshipper's response to God's Word, prayer and praise, are frequently mingled; each may find expression in the other's normal form. A hymn may be the vehicle of prayer; praise is expressed in adoration and thanksgiving as well as in song. But song, as K. L. Parry maintains, 'is the more natural expression of collective praise.' Hence 'it is supremely in the hymn of praise that we unite with the universal Church, in heaven and on earth, to magnify the grace and glory of God.'[2]

Hymns telling of individual experience, exhorting to kindness and good works, calling sinners to repentance, may well have their place in a revival service or an evangelistic campaign. But the primary purpose of the hymn as a liturgical form is the praise of Almighty God. In public worship therefore, as Parry rightly insists, 'hymns should be addressed to God and not to men.'[3] This fact is emphasized in the original Latin of the *Te Deum*. A literal translation would be:

> *Thee,* as God, we praise;
> *Thee,* as the Lord, we acknowledge;
> *Thee,* the Father everlasting, all the earth doth worship . . .

The purpose of worship is to turn our attention from ourselves to God. We assemble and meet together not primarily to bring our needs to God, nor primarily to seek strength for coming days, but first and foremost to set forth God's most worthy praise, to give unto the Lord the glory due

[1] K. L. Parry, op. cit., pp. 239-40. I am much indebted to Mr. Parry's essay in this section.
[2] ibid., p. 239.
[3] ibid., p. 228.

unto His name. The supreme importance of worship is that in it man attains his chief end of glorifying God.[1] Praise, therefore, is its characteristic note just as the Eucharist is its norm; and the medium of praise is the hymn.

2. *An Act of Prayer.* A second and lesser use of the hymn is as a medium of prayer. It may express Adoration:

> My God, how wonderful Thou art,
> Thy majesty how bright. . . .

Or Invocation:

> Light up this house with glory, Lord,
> Enter and claim Thine own. . . .

It may be the medium of Confession and Supplication:

> Oh, how shall I, whose native sphere
> Is dark, whose mind is dim,
> Before the Ineffable appear,
> And on my naked spirit bear
> The uncreated beam?

> Dear Lord and Father of mankind,
> Forgive our feverish ways;
> Reclothe us in our rightful mind,
> In purer lives Thy service find,
> In deeper reverence praise.

Or of Thanksgiving:

> For peaceful homes and healthful days,
> For all the blessings earth displays,
> We owe Thee thankfulness and praise,
> Who givest all.

Or again of Intercession:

> When wilt Thou save the people,
> O God of mercy, when? . . .

[1] 'It is often said that worship is a preparation for life. It would perhaps be truer to say that life is a preparation for worship.'—K. L. Parry, op. cit., p. 230.

O hear us when we cry to Thee
For those in peril on the sea.

The Commemoration of the Faithful Departed is finely expressed in such hymns as:

Come let us join our friends above
That have obtained the prize. . . .

For all the saints who from their labours rest .

As a Prayer of Illumination, what can rival:

Come, Holy Ghost, for moved by Thee
The prophets wrote and spoke;
Unlock the truth, Thyself the key,
Unseal the sacred Book.

Finally, Wesley and Watts have each given us a moving expression of Oblation:

Ready for all Thy perfect will,
Our acts of faith and love repeat;
Till death Thine endless mercies seal,
And make the sacrifice complete.

Were the whole realm of nature mine,
That were a present far too small;
Love, so amazing, so divine
Demands my soul, my life, my all.

Sung with reverence and sincerity, such hymns become the channels of fervent corporate prayer.

3. *A Confession of Faith.* In the third place, a hymn may be used as a confession of faith, a declaration of the mighty acts of God in Creation and Redemption and Providence, a setting forth of the things most surely believed among us. This function of the hymn may be combined with either or both of the others; indeed the greatest hymns evoke praise by a contemplation of the central facts of the faith. John Henry Newman's 'Praise to the Holiest in the

height' is a classic example. It is to Watts and Wesley, however, that the greatest debt is owed. The hymns of both are rich in dogmatic content, setting forth as they do the great doctrines of the Christian faith. Isaac Watts's subjects, for instance, are not sunsets and mountain peaks, whispering woods and babbling brooks; they are the central beliefs of our holy religion. Each article of the Apostles' Creed has a place in his hymns:

> He built the earth, He spread the sky,
> And fixed the starry lights on high :

'I believe in God the Father Almighty, Maker of heaven and earth.'

> He sent His Son with power to save
> From guilt, and darkness, and the grave :

'And in Jesus Christ His only Son our Lord.'

> Through this vain world He guides our feet,
> And leads us to His holy seat :

'I believe in the Holy Ghost.'

> Come let us join our cheerful songs
> With angels round the throne :

'The Holy Catholic Church; the Communion of Saints.'

> His power subdues our sins;
> And His forgiving love,
> Far as the east is from the west,
> Doth all our guilt remove :

'The Forgiveness of sins.'

> They go from strength to strength
> Through this dark vale of tears,
> Till each arrives at length,
> Till each in heaven appears ;

O glorious seat,
 When God our King
 Shall thither bring
Our willing feet!

'The Resurrection of the body, And the life everlasting. Amen.'

The classic English Free Churches—Baptist, Congregational, Presbyterian and Methodist—stand in the central dogmatic tradition of Christendom; they hold the full Catholic Apostolic Faith—the faith of the whole Church. This faith should be declared in our worship, and here is the confessional use of the hymn: our creed, if not *said,* may be *sung.* When we are true to our own tradition of hymnody, the Catholic Faith that we hold is embodied in the permanent liturgical structure of our worship by being set forth in our corporate praise.

CHAPTER VI

The Sacraments

I VISIBLE WORDS

THE central act of the Marriage Service is the giving and receiving of a ring. The ring does not constitute the marriage. The pledging of their troth by bridegroom and bride, in a prescribed form of words, is all that is legally required. But the ring is an outward and visible sign which seals the promise that has been made. The promise, the pledged word, is the vital thing; but the ring expresses that word in a visible form. For the rest of her life the woman wears it, and it is a constant reminder to them both of their pledge of fidelity and love. It is for husband and wife a visible word.

What the ring is for the bride, the Sacraments are for the Church: they are signs and seals of the promises of God.[1] They 'represent invisible things in a manner adapted to our weak capacity, and the spiritual truth, which is at once figured and exhibited by the signs.'[2] 'They present Christ the more clearly to us. . . . For Baptism testifies that we are washed and purified; the Supper of the Eucharist that we are redeemed.'[3] Since therefore they set forth the Word

[1] Calvin defines a Sacrament as 'an outward sign wherewith the Lord sealeth to our consciences the promises of His good will toward us, to sustain the weakness of our faith'—*Institutes* IV, xiv, 1,

[2] Calvin, op. cit., IV. xvii. 11,

[3] ibid., IV, xiv, 22,

made flesh, Baptism and the Lord's Supper are, in St. Augustine's phrase, *verba visibilia*—'visible words.'

Such a definition at once places the Sacraments at the very heart of Christian Worship, depending as this does upon the Christian revelation. The divine Word, to which worship is the response, is set forth in the Scripture Lessons, the Sermon, the Creed (when used), the Liturgy (whether a 'set form' or the 'sung liturgy' of hymns), and also in its dramatic presentation in Baptism and the Lord's Supper. Together with the Bible and Preaching, therefore, the Sacraments are one of the primary 'modes' of the Word since they embody and set forth the Gospel. Christian worship thus consists of the fusion of two elements, something spoken (*legomenon*) and something done (*drōmenon*); both being the embodiment of, and response to, the same divine Word of revelation and redemption. But the second depends upon the first: the Word spoken and heard is primary; the Word acted and visible is its sign and seal.[1] The Sacraments do not stand alone. Calvin, for whom they meant everything, is the first to admit that, apart from the apprehension of a promise, a Sacrament is as void and empty as a seal hanging on a parchment that has nothing written on it.[2] And he observes that the penitent thief on the cross became the brother of believers even though he never partook of the Lord's Supper.[3] Calvin, whose great desire was the restoration of weekly Communion, is not the one to minimize, much less decry, the Sacraments; he is logical if nothing else. He is merely viewing them in their true perspective as

[1] 'Protestantism proclaims, not a Gospel of sacraments, but sacraments of the Gospel'—N. Micklem, *Christian Worship*, p. 245.

[2] *Institutes*, IV. xiv. 4-5.

[3] ibid., IV. xvi. 31.

signs and seals of the Word. 'The Word, and the Word alone,' says Luther, 'is the vehicle of grace.' Hence, as Nathaniel Micklem observes, 'the Sacraments convey grace because they are modes of the Word.'[1]

Two things follow from this. First, because the Sacraments embody and set forth the Gospel of God's pardon and grace, the vital thing in them is God's action and not man's experience. 'It belongs to our tradition and to the truth of the Gospel to lay all the stress upon the action of the living God. It is God who calls and regenerates, He who comes and gives Himself to us. His action is first and last; our worship is but *Antwort* to His *Wort*, an answer to His Word.'[2] The emphasis in Baptism is not upon *our* presentation and dedication of the child or even on *our* faith, but upon God's sovereign regenerating grace. The efficacy of the Holy Communion is not to be measured by the intensity of *our* emotional experience at the Table of the Lord; it is *Christ* who imparts Himself to us through the medium of the broken bread and poured out wine. That is not to say that man's part in the Sacraments is unimportant; it is to reassert the biblical affirmation of classical Protestantism that in the work of our salvation God's action alone is primary and what man does is always secondary. 'By grace are ye saved through faith; and that not of yourselves: it is the gift of God' (Eph. ii. 8).

Secondly, because our redemption was accomplished through the death and resurrection of Christ, it is His redeeming Work which gives their meaning to the Gospel Sacraments. They consist essentially of action; and their action, as Forsyth says, 'is symbolical of Christ's Act, not of

[1] op. cit., p. 243.
[2] ibid.

His essence.'[1] Grace is conveyed, that is to say, not through the elements as such, but through the sacramental action to which they are integral. Thus 'the efficacy of Baptism is not in water but in washing, of the Communion not in bread but in bread *broken*.'[2] The Sacraments are therefore essentially *dramatic;* their essence is *action;* they are by their very nature sacred *rites*. And their ritual action may not be minimized or eliminated without radically altering their character and obscuring their evangelical meaning. When our Lord broke the bread and took into His hands the cup, He bade His disciples, not merely to contemplate His acts, but to repeat them: 'This *do* . . .'

Classical Protestantism, no less than classical Catholicism, has always maintained that the Sacraments are not mere symbols (in the modern sense of the word) but means of grace: they convey what they symbolize. 'They are the acts of God in His Church, whereby that *opus operatum* of Christ, never to be repeated, is, as it were, extended and brought home to believers.'[3] This has been lucidly expressed by J. S. Whale:

The Sacraments do not add anything to the Word, any more than the kiss and the ring add anything to plighted troth. But they do movingly reiterate it; they give effect to it. 'They be certain sure witnesses and effectual signs of grace, and God's good will towards us, by the which he doth work invisibly in us, and doth not only quicken but also strengthen our Faith in him.' These familiar words from the Thirty-nine Articles, closely based on the Augsburg Confession, testify that the Sacraments do verily mediate God's grace. They are more than mere remembrances of heavenly things; the Church would be capable of such remembrances without Sacraments.

[1] P. T. Forsyth, *The Church and the Sacraments,* p. 233.
[2] N. Micklem, op. cit., p. 245.
[3] ibid., p. 244.

They are signs whereby the Holy Spirit inwardly affects us. Like the printed score of the *Fifth Symphony,* through which the music in Beethoven's mind is mediated to successive generations, so the Sacraments are 'conveyances'; sign and effect coincide; the score is played and the music heard; so, God himself sacramentally unites the symbolic action and the grace which it conveys.[1]

Before considering Baptism and the Holy Communion in greater detail, the uniqueness of these two Gospel Sacraments must be stressed. Five other so-called sacraments, found in the medieval Church, are retained in the Church of Rome—Confirmation, Penance, Orders, Matrimony and Extreme Unction. The Reformers, however, insisted that these 'are not to be counted for Sacraments of the Gospel' since they 'have not like nature of Sacraments with Baptism, and the Lord's Supper, for that they have not any visible sign or ceremony ordained of God.' 'There are two Sacraments ordained of Christ our Lord in the Gospels, that is to say, Baptism and the Supper of the Lord.'[2] While not denying a 'sacramental' significance to the other medieval rites, therefore, we shall do well to reserve the term 'Sacrament' for these two. They alone can claim dominical authority, each of them being based upon a command and a promise of our Lord.

II BAPTISM

From the earliest times Baptism has been the rite of initiation into the Christian Church.[3] On the day of Pentecost three thousand converts were baptized (Acts ii. 38-41).

[1] *Christian Doctrine,* pp. 159-60.
[2] Quotations from Article XXV of the Anglican *Articles of Religion.*
[3] 'Baptism is a sign of initiation by which we are received into the fellowship of the Church, that, being grafted into Christ, we may be numbered among the children of God.' Calvin, *Institutes,* IV. xv. 1.

So, later, were the Ethiopian eunuch (Acts viii. 36-38), Cornelius and his company (Acts x. 47-48), the Philippian jailor and his household (Acts xvi. 33). Baptism is therefore 'the sacrament of regeneration, of the new birth; it marks the distinction between the Church and the world, the end of the journey to Christ, the beginning of the life in Christ.'[1]

No particular mode of Baptism is laid down in the New Testament. St. Paul clearly refers to Baptism by immersion when he speaks of Christians being buried with Christ by Baptism into death and raised up with Him into newness of life (Rom. vi. 3-5). But the linguistic usage of the New Testament provides no grounds for regarding immersion as the only proper mode. The Greek word *baptizō* can mean 'to dip' or 'to immerse'; but it may also mean 'to bathe' or 'to wash' (e.g. Mk. vii. 4; Heb. ix. 10). Indeed, in Lk. xi. 38 it refers to washing of the hands only (cf. Matt. xv. 2 and Mk. vii. 2 and 3). An examination of its use in the New Testament shows clearly that the main idea of the word is 'to wash,' but the precise mode of washing implied is not always the same. In practice Baptism by pouring, or effusion, seems to have been allowed as an alternative to immersion.

The Baptism of adult converts is practised in all the classic branches of the Christian Church. But what of children? Here is the point of cleavage in Protestantism. The Baptist denomination refuses to baptize infants upon what it considers to be adequate Scriptural grounds; the other classic Protestant Churches not only retain the ancient practice of Infant Baptism[2] but attach great evangelical significance to it.

[1] N. Micklem, op. cit., p. 246.

[2] Sometimes called Paedo-baptism.

The issue cannot be decided by a simple appeal to the New Testament evidence. This, it must be admitted, is inconclusive. There is no conclusive historical evidence in the New Testament that children were baptized in the Apostolic Church. The justification of Infant Baptism is ultimately, as Micklem points out, theological rather than historical. But, on the other hand, there is no conclusive New Testament evidence that children were not baptized; and there are at least some grounds for believing that they were. The New Testament data are summarized in *The Report of the Commission on the Sacraments of Baptism and the Lord's Supper* published by the Congregational Union of England and Wales:

> As the New Testament reflects the pioneer stage of missionary activity, the Baptism of which it speaks is naturally that of adult converts for whom it was the dramatic symbol of a radical experience. We read, indeed, of whole families being baptized at the conversion of the head of the family (Acts xvi. 15, 33; 1 Cor. i. 16; xvi. 15), and it seems unnecessary to suppose that all these households were childless. The New Testament thus does not afford sufficient evidence to enable us to say with certainty whether Infant Baptism was already practised. It is sometimes urged by those who today are opposed to Infant Baptism that the custom of the first Christian centuries shows that Infant Baptism did not exist in New Testament times. But here, too, the evidence is indecisive. The child was less prominent in the ancient East than in the modern West, and passages which bear on the question of Infant Baptism are naturally few. . . .
>
> Baptism was regarded from the first as a rite similar to that of circumcision (Rom. iv. 11, and Col. ii. 11, 12), and circumcision was administered to the infants of Jewish parents. Circumcision was, indeed, restricted, like other Jewish ordinances, to males. But in Christ Jesus there is neither male nor female (Gal. iii. 28), and it is not improbable that the infants of Chris-

tian parents, whether male or female, were from the first baptized. Whether that be so or not, it is clear that St. Paul regarded the children of Christian parents as belonging to the Christian community, that sphere over which Christ reigned and in which the grace of God was experienced (cp. 1 Cor. vii. 14, where the children of the Christian mother are described as 'clean'). It is in this that we today find part of the meaning of Infant Baptism.[1]

What then is the significance of Baptism? Two popular misconceptions claim a brief reference. First, Baptism is not dedication. The two things are poles apart in nature and emphasis. 'At a Dedication Service it is the parents who are the agents, at a Baptism it is Christ through His Church; at a Dedication Service it is the parents who declare what they will do, at a Baptism it is Christ Who through His representative, the minister, takes the child in His arms and declares what He has done and will do for the child; at a Dedication Service it is the parents who promise, at a Baptism it is Christ.'[2]

Secondly, Baptism is not a confession of faith. It may well be the occasion of a confession of faith; indeed, apart from faith it has no efficacy. Both adults and children are baptized into the household of faith—the confessing Church. But it is God's grace, not man's faith, which is signified in Baptism. The symbolism of washing sets forth God's action—not ours. Herein lies the justification of Infant Baptism.

The great and world-wide denomination of Baptists is so named because its members rightly insist that to be a Christian a man or woman must be a believer. . . . Thus the Baptists

[1] pp. 4-5.

[2] N. Micklem, op. cit., p. 250.

recognize no other baptism than that which they administer to candidates who have reached years of discretion. They argue that to baptize a helpless infant only a few weeks old, who is obviously incapable of the responsive faith of the believer, is meaningless and worse. To this the universal tradition of Christendom replies, not of course by belittling faith in an adult who seeks baptism, but by insisting on our redemption as an objective fact just at that point in human life where no subjective response to it is possible on the part of the baptized individual.[1]

Baptism therefore signifies that grace comes before faith. Our standing before God is on the basis, not of what we do, but of what He has done. Our prayer is that He will accept us, 'not weighing our merits, but pardoning our offences.' 'By grace are ye saved through faith; and that not of yourselves: it is the gift of God: not of works, lest any man should boast' (Eph. ii. 8-9).

This fact of salvation by grace alone, not dependent upon the good works of man but the sheer gift of God, is the central theme of Holy Scripture. 'All is of God. This divine initiative in redemption is the characteristic thought not only of Paul the great apostle of Grace, but also of the whole Bible. Grace means love in action; love which takes the initiative, invasively and creatively. "While we were yet sinners, Christ died for us." '[2] The whole story of the Old Testament is the story of God's free, unmerited grace to Israel. They were a chosen people, but not through any merits of their own. God did not choose this particular nation to be the instrument of His self-revelation to the world because they were better than other nations; or because they were more responsive to His call; or yet because

[1] J. S. Whale, op. cit., p. 165.

[2] J. S. Whale, op. cit., p. 77.

they could be depended upon to fulfil His redemptive purpose in the earth. He chose them as an act of grace. Far from being responsive and obedient to the divine will, the whole history of this people is a story of continual apostasy and rebellion. Yet God never cast them off. Though they failed Him, God never failed them: though they slighted and dishonoured Him, He was still their Saviour and mighty Deliverer.

The relationship of God to His ancient People was a covenant relationship. That is, they were bound together by an agreement, a marriage bond, in which each pledged his fidelity and love. But this covenant was a covenant of grace.[1] God took Israel for His bride, as it were; and He took her for better and for worse. Israel might forget Him, but God's mercy never failed. His People might be unfaithful, but God's Word remained sure; so that they had to say: 'He hath not dealt with us after our sins; nor rewarded us according to our iniquities.'

But this Word of God's grace to His People, this covenant of grace under which they lived, was sealed by a ritual act—the rite of circumcision. This was the outward and visible sign by which it was kept continually before their eyes. The Israelite child did not remain outside the covenant until he chose to enter it on reaching years of discretion. It was his inalienable birthright. A rich heritage was his, not because he had earned it, but because God had freely bestowed it upon the People into which he was born. And his circumcision when eight days old was the sign and seal of this fact. It marked him as a member of the Covenant People of God.

[1] For a full discusion of the Covenant see my book, *The Nature and Authority of the Bible* (James Clarke), chapter VI. ii. 1.

When we turn from the Old Testament to the New, we find this same theme writ large. Man is brought to God by God coming to man. In a Carpenter of Nazareth the God of all grace has visited and redeemed His people. And in the parable of the Labourers in the Vineyard (Matt. xx. 1-16) Jesus shows that divine grace, and not human works, forms the basis of our relationship with God.

Here is the story of the sheer generosity of an employer who, out of pity for the unemployed, pays the same wage to those who have worked for one hour as to those who have laboured all the day. But to understand it we must see it in its setting. The disciples had just seen a rich young man go sorrowfully away because he could not forgo the possessions which stood between himself and discipleship. Then, through Peter, they ask what shall be their reward; they have done that from which this young man shrank—'Behold, we have forsaken all, and followed thee; what shall we have therefore?' It is this question which calls forth the parable. Jesus first of all assures them that they, and all others who have made sacrifice for Christ's sake, shall receive an abundant reward; but He goes on to show them that this is not a question which the disciple should ask. It savoured too much of self-complacency. It revealed an attitude of spirit which regarded its own service as having the right to claim a reward. He would teach Peter and his brethren that this neat little theology of the counting-house with its exact balance of merit and recompense has no place in the economy of God. Men are accepted by Him, not on the ground of anything they have done, but because of the bounty of God. Salvation is by grace alone; not of works, lest any man should boast.

Just as in the life of the Old Israel God's Word of grace

found visible expression in an institution, the rite of circumcision, so also in the life of the New Israel, the Christian Church, it is sealed in the sacrament of Baptism. Herein lies the justification of the Baptism of children. In Infant Baptism salvation by grace alone is portrayed as it is portrayed nowhere else in the life of the Church. By administering Baptism just at that time when the one receiving it can make no personal response, we declare that the grace of God comes before the faith of man; that it is by virtue of that grace, not of anything which he can do, that this child, and all men, are redeemed; that God in His grace has provided in Christ the means of our redemption without consulting us or asking our permission, and provided it for us, not only before we were old enough to know anything about it, but before we had a being. Infant Baptism thus declares and exhibits before the eyes of the Church, as nothing else can declare and exhibit, the fact that God's provision for our sin has an objective existence which is quite independent of our response to it; that Christ is the Lamb slain from the foundation of the world. As B. L. Manning puts it, 'Every time we baptise a child, we declare to the whole world in the most solemn manner that God does for us what He does without our merits and even without our knowledge. In baptism, perhaps more plainly than anywhere else, God commends His love toward us in that *while we were yet sinners* Christ died for us.'[1]

Baptism is thus a sign and seal of the covenant of grace. It stands in the same relationship to the new covenant as does circumcision to the old.

Christ died for us, and out of His work arose the Church. Out of and into the fellowship of the Church are all the children

[1] *Why not Abandon the Church?* p. 47.

of believers born. They may have as yet neither sin nor faith of their own; it will be necessary for them later of their own consent to take up their inheritance in Christ and His Church, but their inheritance it is, as in fact it is not the inheritance of the heathen. Some men are born free, some attain freedom at a great price; the children of the Church are born free. No one may say without blasphemy that God loves some children more than others or deny that Christ has died for all, but the Baptism of infants corresponds with spiritual facts, that the children of the Church are born into the Christian inheritance, and that the promises of God to Christians are not to them only but to their seed after them.[1]

It follows that Baptism may properly be administered to the children of believers only, as the *Savoy Declaration* of 1658 so emphatically declares.[2] R. W. Dale, however, maintained that since Baptism is a sign of the finished work of Christ who died for all men, it should not be withheld from any child.[3] This position has become generally accepted among Free Churchmen during the last half century, but the resulting widespread practice of indiscriminate Baptism has virtually emptied the sacrament of its significance as the door into the Church. The Puritans strove to eliminate the idea that the Church is coterminous with the nation; their successors, ironically enough, have succumbed to a practice which implies precisely this. The wheel has turned full circle. The solution is far from simple, as every conscientious minister knows full well. Is he to refuse a Christian ceremony to any parents who sincerely desire it for their child? When every allowance has been made for

[1] N. Micklem, op. cit., p. 249.

[2] See *Sav. Decl.*, ch. XXIX. iv.

[3] *Manual of Congregational Principles,* Book III, chapter ii, pp. 126ff.

superstitious and quasi-magical conceptions of the sacrament, the vestigial Christianity of large sections of the population, who are out of touch with the regular life and worship of the churches, must be reckoned with. Discrimination is notoriously difficult, to say the least. Who precisely are the children of believers, and who are not? The obvious criterion is full communicant membership of the Church. But can we deny some measure of Christian belief to any parent who sincerely desires Christian Baptism for his or her child?

The crux of the matter is surely that unless the child is really received into the fellowship of the Church and brought up in the faith of the Church, Baptism is meaningless. Where the parents are communicant members of the household of faith, their pledges should be sufficient. But what of the children of those who desire Christian Baptism for their little ones but who are not themselves within the fellowship of the Church? Can any pledges of theirs suffice if, as all too frequently happens, they are not to darken the doors of a church until the arrival of the next child? The answer, it would seem, is ultimately pastoral rather than liturgical. If our present practice is to be continued, two things are necessary to ensure that Baptism does not become an 'empty' sign. First, parents must be instructed in the meaning of the sacrament and the obligations that it places upon them. Here is a fruitful field for evangelism. Secondly, when neither of the parents is a communicant member of the Church, sponsors chosen from the communicant membership are needed to accept responsibility for bringing the child into the fellowship of the Church and instructing him or her in the Christian faith.

In either case, it will be necessary for the child, on reaching years of discretion, to confirm[1] his or her membership of the Christian community before being admitted to the privileges and responsibilities of full communicant membership. Only then is Baptism completed, the sovereign grace of God which it sets forth being met by the personal response of faith: 'By grace are ye saved through faith.'[2]

Baptism, as the sacrament of initiation into the Christian Church, should be administered at a full service of the Church and not privately, except in cases of extreme necessity.[3] The usual time is at the morning service after either the New Testament Lesson or the Sermon. It may, however, fittingly take place at the beginning of worship. During the singing of a baptismal hymn, the minister proceeds to the font to which the baptismal party has been brought. Matt. xxviii. 18-20 and Mk. x. 13-16 are read and the meaning of the sacrament set forth in a brief exhortation. The parents, or sponsors, are then asked to make profession of their faith and promise to instruct the child in the truths and duties of the Christian faith and to bring him or her up in the nurture and admonition of the Lord and in the fellowship of the Church. Prayer is now offered, which should

[1] In the traditional rite of Confirmation the emphasis is upon God's action, not man's. It is the confirmation not of a baptismal vow but of a person—i.e. the strengthening of a person by the gift of the Holy Spirit. The Book of Common Prayer, however, rightly insists upon a renewal of baptismal vows as an essential condition: 'children being now come to the years of discretion' must 'ratify and confirm the same.' See the Preface of The Order of Confirmation.

[2] Concerning the relationship of Baptism and Confirmation, D. E. W. Harrison says, 'Only in so far as both are still regarded as essentially one is it possible theologically to do justice to the real meaning of either.' op. cit., p. 111.

[3] If for an urgent reason Baptism is administered privately, some representatives of the Church should be present with the minister. This applies also to clinical Communions.

include an invocation of the Holy Spirit (*epiklēsis*) to sanctify the child to be baptized and the water to its holy use, after which the minister and people say together the Lord's Prayer. Then the congregation is asked to stand as a sign that they receive this child in the name of the Lord; the minister, receiving the child from the father, enquires his or her name; and water is poured or sprinkled on the child's head in the name of the Father, and of the Son, and of the Holy Ghost. After blessing the child, the minister declares him or her to be received into the household of faith and charges the congregation to pray that he or she may be nurtured and grow strong and continue Christ's faithful servant unto life's end. The child is then given back to the mother with a brief charge to the parents, a post-baptismal prayer is offered and the minister either proceeds with the Order for Public Worship or dismisses the congregation with the Blessing.

III THE LORD'S SUPPER

As Baptism marks the beginning of the Christian life, so the Lord's Supper provides for its continuance. It is the supreme means of grace: here, as nowhere else, God gives Himself to man; here, as nowhere else, man may offer himself to God. In this sacrament 'we accept that which God gives, become that which He makes of us (by grace, not by merit), and render it up to Him. Worship is here that which ideally it must be—the return to God of that which came from God.'[1] For this reason the Lord's Supper is the central act of Christian worship. Nothing else can

[1] C. H. Dodd, 'The Sacrament of the Lord's Supper in the New Testament,' *Christian Worship* (ed. N. Micklem), p. 82.

compare with it. It links us by an unbroken chain of witness to the Upper Room itself; it lifts us out of time into the heavenly places to partake of the marriage supper of the Lamb.

> And thus that dark betrayal night
> With the last advent we unite,
> By one blest chain of loving rite,
> Until He come.

In this rite there is gathered up all the riches of our Christian heritage.

> There is first the backward look to the Last Supper and to Calvary—'in memory of Me'; there is, second, the forward look to 'the bridal Supper of the Lamb' in the perfected Kingdom—'till He come'; there is, third, the feeding upon Christ by faith—'take, eat, this is My body'; there is, fourth, the Church as the Body of Christ—'as My Father hath sent Me, so send I you'; fifth, the rite is Eucharistic, the Church's thanksgiving in the confession of the Redeemer's Name, *sacrificium laudis;* it is *sacrificium propitiatorium* only as it may mystically be regarded as an extension of the Passion into time. Above and before all there is the Real Presence of the Lord Himself as surely as on that last betrayal night, sealing His promise to believers and giving Himself unto His own.[1]

The Lord's Supper, however, does not stand alone. It is the climax of Christian worship; a Sacrament of the Word; a sign and seal of the Gospel contained in Holy Scripture, declared in the Sermon, confessed in hymns and creed. 'It is the Gospel in the action which makes the action a sacrament.'[2] The principle of the indivisibility of Word and Sacrament lies at the very heart of Reformed worship. 'The true ministration of the Sacrament,' says Calvin, 'standeth

[1] N. Micklem, op. cit., p. 252.

[2] P. Carnegie Simpson, *The Evangelical Church Catholic*, p. 85.

not without the Word.' As Nathaniel Micklem points out, 'this does not necessarily imply that there can be no celebration of Baptism or the Supper without preaching, but that except in a community where the Word is faithfully preached and heartily accepted there can be no true Christian Sacraments.'[1] The service of Holy Communion consists therefore of two main parts, the 'liturgy of the Word' preceding and leading up to the 'liturgy of the Upper Room.'[2] The latter, the Supper proper, is not to be regarded as a separate act of worship, much less as an appendix to a 'preaching' service. Word and Sacrament together constitute an organic whole. For this reason there should be no break between the two. Non-communicant worshippers may leave during the singing of a hymn, or while the organist improvises at its close, and elders or deacons take their places at the Lord's Table.

The celebration of the Supper must be considered therefore in the setting of the full act of worship of which it is the climax. The Communion office as a whole consists of four closely related sections. First, there is the approach in praise and penitence. Second, there is the ministry of the Word in Scripture Lessons and Sermon with intercession and praise. This completes the first part of the service, what Maxwell calls the 'liturgy of the Word.' The third section of the office is characterized by thanksgiving and oblation through the participation of the worshippers in the words and action of the Upper Room. In the fourth they unite in the final act of communion through the delivery and reception of the bread and wine.

[1] op. cit., p. 253.
[2] In ancient liturgical usage they are called the 'liturgy of the catechumens' and the 'liturgy of the faithful.'

The structure and contents of the 'liturgy of the Word' have already been discussed.[1] We turn now to consider the 'liturgy of the Upper Room' which comprises the third and fourth sections of the Communion office. It is essentially action. 'Central to the whole is the re-enactment of what took place in the Upper Room.'[2] Its form is Scriptural, being determined by the New Testament narratives of institution, especially the earliest in 1 Cor. xi. 23-25. In these accounts we find what Dom Gregory Dix describes as a seven-action scheme: 'Our Lord (1) took bread: (2) "gave thanks" over it: (3) broke it: (4) distributed it saying certain words; later He (5) took a cup: (6) "gave thanks" over that: (7) handed it to His disciples, saying certain words.'[3] As Dix points out, in liturgical usage these seven actions are reproduced as four, the bread and wine being taken together at each stage. Every classic liturgy therefore has four great actions answering to those of our Lord in the Upper Room: 'He took,' 'He gave thanks,' 'He brake,' and 'He gave.' These, together with the Words of Institution which are their warrant, are integral parts of the sacrament, which is incomplete if any one of them is omitted. In so far as Scripture is our norm, we may not leave out or minimize any part of the symbolic action which is the very essence of this rite.

This fact cannot be too strongly emphasized among Free Churchmen today. Celebrations of the Lord's Supper which are gravely defective are all too common in many of our churches. The reason is not far to seek. In our ministerial

[1] See chapters III and IV.

[2] E. R. Micklem, *Our Approach to God,* p. 261.

[3] *The Shape of the Liturgy,* p. 48. The reference in (6) is to the Synoptic accounts which mention a separate thanksgiving over the cup.

training—admirable enough in Biblical Exegesis, Church History, Systematic Theology and Homiletics—there has been an almost complete neglect of Liturgics. The Anglican ordinand, whose Prayer Book provides him with a complete liturgy, is well trained in liturgical principles and history; the Free Church minister, who is responsible for ordering the worship which he conducts, more often than not leaves college with little or no knowledge of the theology of worship or of the rich liturgical heritage of Christendom. Not until our ministers receive an adequate liturgical training will our worship be worthy of our own great traditions.

But defective celebrations of the Supper do not always indicate ministerial incompetence; they may be the result of an arbitrary over-emphasis on some one part of the rite to the virtual exclusion of other parts. A striking example of this kind of over-emphasis occurs in J. Alan Kay's otherwise excellent book, *The Nature of Christian Worship*. Dr. Kay, whom no one could accuse of liturgical ignorance, virtually limits the significant action of the Lord's Supper to the worshippers' reception of the elements. This, he tells us, was the particular emphasis of Jesus Himself:

No doubt He went through all the usual ritual accompaniments, whether it was a Chaburah supper or some other kind of meal; but He did not draw attention to them all. No doubt He 'took bread'; but it is questionable whether He intended us to stress that action and turn it into an offertory. No doubt He 'gave thanks'; but He did not draw special attention to it, or interpret it as anything other than the usual grace before meat, though it would have been very easy for Him to have done so. No doubt He broke the bread; but there is no sign that His doing so was any more than the usual necessary preliminary to its distribution. . . . The thing that He made to stand out, and to which He drew special attention, was the eating of the bread and the drinking of the wine; it was 'this' that they had to 'do.'

And he concludes: 'We must, therefore, surely base the meaning of our service upon this eating and drinking and the interpretation that Jesus put upon them; and to emphasize the other things as though they were equally important is to misconceive the meaning and purpose of what was done.'[1]

The crucial question is: Did our Lord single out the eating of the bread and drinking of the wine for special emphasis? Was it only this that He commanded His disciples to do? If so, why has the rite been known from the earliest times as 'the *breaking* of bread'? Let P. T. Forsyth reply: 'The exact point of the Lord's Supper,' he says, 'is that *such symbolism did not lie in the elements but in the action*, the entire action—word and deed. . . . It was the *action* that was symbolical, the breaking rather than the bread, the outpouring rather than the wine.'[2] 'In the rite there are three centres of interest—the elements, His act, their act. But the ruling thing is not the elements but the act. And it is His act, not theirs, that is in the foreground. He did something, gave; they did something and took.'[3]

If it be objected that this dramatic conception of the sacrament opens the door to what is popularly (though inaccurately) called 'ritualism,' the answer is that it is Protestant to the core. It was precisely because classic Protestantism insisted upon taking the New Testament seriously that it refused to regard the Lord's Supper in terms of the conse-

1 pp. 90-91.

2 *The Church and the Sacraments,* p. 234.

3 ibid., p. 248.

crated elements alone. It is the Roman Catholic who finds the essence of the sacrament in the elements; and it is its failure to give precedence to the action of the Supper that Forsyth calls the lame foot of Anglicanism.[1] E. R. Micklem is stating the classic Nonconformist position when he writes: 'Without claiming that there should be absolute uniformity either in the structure or in the language of the service, we can confidently affirm that there are various acts to be performed which no presiding minister should feel free to omit, and, moreover, that these acts will largely determine the structure of the service if any regard is paid to dramatic unity. They belong to the essential meanings of the rite.'[2]

In the action of the Lord's Supper there are four great acts in which the worshipping Church recalls the acts of Christ in the Upper Room.

1. *The Offertory,* in which the people's gifts and more especially the elements of bread and wine are presented at the Lord's Table, corresponds to our Lord's first act: 'He took bread.' No other part of the Supper has been subject to more change. It was originally the solemn presentation of the people's free-will offerings, not of money but in kind—the fruits of the earth, the symbols of their toil and God's blessing—as a token of the consecration of themselves and all their possessions to the service of God.[3] As Gore observes,

[1] ibid., p. 234, Note 1.

[2] op. cit., p. 259.

[3] 'Underlying this practice was the conception of the Eucharist as the Church's thank-offering for the blessings of Creation and Redemption. The gifts of the earth, redeemed in their use by the new Christian outlook, were offered as first-fruits to God as an act of homage and acknowledgement of His dominion and of the fact that all that we have comes from Him'—J. H. Srawley, 'The Holy Communion Service' in *Liturgy and Worship,* p. 318.

'Early canons suggest that a Christian Eucharist in the first age must have frequently resembled a modern harvest thanksgiving.'[1] From these gifts of the congregation, offered at the Lord's Table, sufficient bread and wine were set apart by the minister for the celebration of the sacrament; what remained of the offerings was given to the poor. 'It was only later that the act of oblation was concentrated in the prayer of consecration and confined to the elements.'[2]

When in course of time a money offering replaced the offerings in kind, the original connection of the people's offering with the bread and wine was obscured. In the Eastern Church, however, the presentation of the eucharistic elements became the chief ceremonial act of the service, the 'Great Entrance.' After the elaborate preparation of the Prothesis in a side chapel,[3] the elements were carried in solemn procession through the north door of the Ikonostasis (the sanctuary screen), down the centre of the church, and back through the Royal Door into the sanctuary to be placed upon the Holy Table for consecration. In the West the process is reversed, the action being simplified. The Offertory in the Mass (the Lesser Oblation) becomes, as Phillips says, a shadow of its old impressive self. 'The people's offering has gone: all that survives is the bringing of the paten and chalice containing the elements by the deacon to the priest, who places them on the altar.'[4] There remain, as relics of the original significance, the Offertory Psalm which was formerly sung during the people's offering and the 'Secret' collect, e.g.:

1 C. Gore, *The Body of Christ,* p. 172.

2 D. E. W. Harrison, *The Book of Common Prayer,* p. 80.

3 See p. 17.

4 C. S. Phillips, *The Background of the Prayer Book,* p. 113.

Hearken, O Lord, to our prayers and graciously accept these offerings of thy servants and handmaids: that what individuals have offered to the honour of thy name, may avail unto all for salvation.[1]

Even these relics disappear in the Reformation rites. Sacrificial language associated with the Great Oblation of the Mass (the offering to God of the consecrated elements as the body and blood of Christ) had come to be used at the Lesser Oblation, as the Offertory was called. The Reformers therefore stripped the Offertory of its prayers and chant, thus reducing it to the simple act of placing the bread and wine upon the Holy Table. In the Book of Common Prayer the Offertory begins with sentences of Scripture emphasizing the duty of giving both for the support of the ministry (oblations) and for the relief of the poor (alms). After the collection of the 'alms' and 'oblations,'[2] they are humbly presented and placed upon the Holy Table together with the bread and wine. Archdeacon Harrison points out that 'the rubrics at the end of the 1549 book provide that the families of the parish shall in turn offer every Sunday, at the time of the Offertory, the just value and price of the holy loaf, and shall also send a member or representative to receive communion. . . . This interesting provision vanished in 1552 when the curate and churchwardens were to provide the bread and wine at the expense

[1] The 'Secret' for the Fifth Sunday after Pentecost. See A. G. Hebert, *Liturgy and Society,* p. 77, quoted by D. E. W. Harrison, op. cit., p. 80.

[2] 'In 1549 the worshippers came into the quire and offered personally into the poor men's box, and in some places a second box was provided for oblations. Historically therefore the word oblation in the English Prayer Book, unlike the Scottish, has no reference to the bread and wine which anciently was the primary reference'—D. E. W. Harrison, op. cit., p. 81.

of the parish.'[1] The original people's offering is preserved at Brasenose College Chapel, Oxford, where the bread and wine are presented by two members of the foundation at the Offertory;[2] and Archdeacon Harrison rightly maintains that 'there is no reason doctrinally why the old connection of the word should not be restored, and the bread and wine, made once again the people's offering, presented at the Lord's Table by representatives of the congregation.'[3]

In the Scottish rite the Offertory Chant reappears as a metrical Psalm, Paraphrase or Hymn sung while the covered elements are brought into the church by the minister and elders and placed on the Holy Table. David Cairns suggests that this Scottish custom may be a relic of the 'Great Entrance' which has come down through the Gallican tradition to the Celtic Church and remained after the Reformation.[4] It seems more likely, however, that it derives from the practice of Geneva.[5] Among the English Puritans the Presbyterians followed this same custom but the Independents and Baptists had the bread and wine placed on the Table before the service began. The elements remained covered during the 'liturgy of the Word'; they were unveiled, and so presented, at the beginning of the 'liturgy of the Upper Room.' This is still the practice of Congregationalists and Baptists. It is also followed by the Methodists who generally use John Wesley's modification of the Anglican rite.

[1] ibid., p. 80.

[2] See J. H. Srawley, 'The Holy Communion Service' in *Liturgy and Worship,* p. 319, Note 1.

[3] op. cit., p. 81.

[4] See 'The Holy Communion in the Presbyterian Church' in *The Holy Communion: A Symposium* (ed. Hugh Martin), p. 80.

[5] See W. D. Maxwell, *An Outline of Christian Worship,* p. 139, Note 2.

The relationship between the presentation of the bread and wine and the people's money offering is frequently obscured in Free Church celebrations of the Lord's Supper by the practice of taking the collection before the Sermon. There is no objection to this in an evening service when the office structure is used. But at the service of Holy Communion the coins in the collection plate represent the offerings in kind from which the bread and wine for the supper were taken and set apart by the minister in the early Church. The Collection should therefore be associated as closely as possible with the presentation of the sacramental elements, whatever form this may take. Which means that its proper place is *after* the Sermon at the beginning of the 'liturgy of the Upper Room.' The offerings should be presented at the Lord's Table and received by the minister who places them on the Table. He should then place the elements also on the Table, if they are brought into the church at this point (as in the Presbyterian custom), or unveil them if they are already on the Table (as in Baptist, Congregationalist and Methodist practice). In this way the unity of the Offertory, as the first part of the action of the Supper, is preserved.

2. *The Prayer of Thanksgiving and Consecration* is derived from our Lord's second action in the Upper Room. 'We read that on the night in which our Lord was betrayed,' says the minister in the English Presbyterian rite, 'He took bread: and, before He brake it He gave thanks to God: Let us in His Name and after His example give God thanks.'[1] It is from this prayer, the *eucharistia,* that the service takes its ancient name—Eucharist.[2] From an early date it as-

[1] See the *Directory for Public Worship* (1921) and *The Presbyterian Service Book* (1948).

[2] The name appears in the *Didache* and in Justin Martyr's *Apology,* both of which belong to the first half of the second century.

sumed a distinctive form since it endeavoured to express all that was implicit in our Lord's own act of thanksgiving. The Eucharistic Prayers of the late third and early fourth centuries have thus a common structure and content, although there are no fixed forms as yet. The Minister first greets the people with the common Christian salutation: 'The Lord be with you'[1]; to which they reply: 'And with thy spirit.' He then bids them: 'Lift up your hearts'; and they respond: 'We lift them up unto the Lord.' This is followed by the exhortation: 'Let us give thanks unto the Lord'; to which the people assent: 'It is meet and right so to do.'[2] The minister then 'praises God as the Creator of all things visible and invisible; the creation passes in an epic procession before the eyes of the worshippers; and there follows the story of the great salvation which God has wrought amid signs and wonders for His people Israel. And like a many-voiced echo of this praise and thanksgiving there sounds forth from the mouths of the congregation the Song of the Cherubim, the "Holy, Holy, Holy" which Isaiah heard in his Vision. But a still more marvellous saving work has God wrought for sinful mankind, in that He has sent His Son, that whosoever believeth on Him might have eternal life. So now the people see unrolled before them the whole drama of redemption, from the birth of the Saviour of the World up to His Ascension and His Second Coming.'[3]

The prayer comes to a burning focus in the memorial of

[1] Or alternatively: 'Peace be with you,' or 'The grace of the Lord Jesus Christ, the love of God, and the communion of the Holy Ghost be with you all.'

[2] Both the Salutation and the *Sursum corda* are first mentioned in the early part of the third century, by which time they seem to have been well established in Christian usage. 'Let us give thanks . . .' is a Jewish form.

[3] F. Heiler, *The Spirit of Worship*, pp. 40-41.

the Passion (*anamnēsis*) which is followed by an invocation of the Holy Spirit (*epiklēsis*) to bless the offerings of bread and wine that they may be the communion of the body and blood of Christ. And since 'in this that the Church offers, she herself is offered to God.'[1] Christians, as the Body of Christ, with these their offerings offer and present themselves (Oblation). There follows the Great Intercession for all sorts and conditions of men, after which minister and people say together the Lord's Prayer.

When fixed forms become normal at the end of the fourth century, they merely crystallize the clearly defined elements in this fluid rite. The ancient dialogue between minister and people—the Salutation and *Sursum corda*—provides the fitting opening of the great Consecration Prayer. Thanksgiving for Creation and Providence is crystallized in the Preface, fixed in the East but variable according to the season of the Christian Year in the West. This is followed by the Hymn of the Cherubim, the *Sanctus,* in which the people join,[2] which leads to remembrance of our Lord's life, death and resurrection, the *Anamnesis,* and thanksgiving for redemption. Then comes invocation of the Holy Spirit, the *Epiclesis,* and Oblation, the offering of the worshippers themselves, collectively and individually, with their sacrifice of praise. Intercession for the living and the dead usually follows, then a doxology, and finally, as the climax, the Lord's Prayer.

This classical form of the Eucharistic Prayer is retained, with certain variations, in the East; in the West it becomes

[1] Augustine, *De Civitate Dei,* x. 6; cf. *Epist.* 272.

[2] The *Sanctus* is mentioned in Clement of Rome's letter to the Corinthians (A.D. 96), see *Epistle* xxxiv. Later it was frequently followed by the *Benedictus qui venit:* 'Blessed is He that cometh in the Name of the Lord. Hosanna in the highest.'

mutilated and distorted in the Roman Canon as a brief summary of the contents of the latter clearly shows. After the Preface (*Vere dignum*), *Sanctus* and *Benedictus qui venit,* the Canon proper begins with a prayer for the acceptance of the gifts and offerings (*Te igitur*) followed by Intercession (*Memento Domine, Communicantes* and *Hanc igitur*). Then comes an invocation for the blessing of the elements (*Quam oblationem*),[1] the recitation of the Words of Institution, an *Anamnesis* (*Unde et memores*), and petition that what has been offered may be acceptable to God (*Supra quae*) and that those who participate may be filled with all heavenly blessing and grace (*Supplices te*). The Canon concludes with intercession for, and memorial of, the dead (*Memento etiam* and *Nobis quoque*) and a doxology.

The primitive Eucharist has been distorted into the medieval sacrifice of the Mass with the result that the Roman Canon is, as Maxwell says, both a dislocation and a fragment.[2] At its heart there is still the Gospel. But the divine initiative is obscured by the human oblation; the service moves from man to God and not from God to man. Hence the emphasis is transferred from the action to the elements and the Mass culminates not in communion but in the miracle of transubstantiation followed by the oblation and adoration of the consecrated bread and wine. The distortion and mutilation of the great Consecration Prayer is the direct result of the perversion of doctrine in the Western Medieval Church. 'Because its doctrine of the Eucharist had ceased to be dynamic; because, strictly speaking, revelation was no longer necessary, the primitive emphasis on the

[1] This is not an *Epiclesis;* there is no invocation of the Holy Spirit.

[2] See *An Outline of Christian Worship,* pp. 59ff.

work of the Holy Spirit was lost. The *Epiklesis* had vanished from the consecration prayer, and in its place is a prayer, earlier certainly than the Middle Ages, that the elements might, by the hand of God's holy angel, be united with the sacrifice of the Heavenly Altar.'[1]

In considering the liturgical results of the Reformation, two things must be borne in mind. First, for the Reformers the medieval view of the Mass as a repetition of the sacrifice of Christ was the supreme abomination. Second, however, they themselves shared the liturgical inheritance of the West. Indeed, with the exception of Cranmer, 'their acquaintance with liturgical forms appears to have been largely restricted to the contemporary Roman forms; of Gallican and Eastern worship they appear to have known almost nothing; and their knowledge of even the primitive worship that they wished to restore was rudimentary and incomplete.'[2] While therefore the Roman Canon received drastic treatment at their hands, their own earlier liturgical achievements were, as Maxwell points out, largely negative: 'they simply omitted what they considered superfluous or incompatible with the new teaching.'

To those who inherit the Reformers' spirit the task yet remains to provide forms broad enough and deep enough for man's whole being to go out to God in adoration, praise, and prayer, and for God's grace to come to man without let or hindrance.

[1] D. E. W. Harrison, op. cit., pp. 44-45. Cf. F. Heiler, *The Spirit of Worship*, p. 65: 'By making the words of institution the central words of the whole Mass, the great prayer of thanksgiving . . . was robbed of its pre-eminent significance, and the *Epiklesis* . . . was deprived of its place.'

[2] W. D. Maxwell, op. cit., pp. 72-73.

To accomplish this requires a bringing forth from the Christian treasury of things both new and old.[1]

Luther, who describes the Canon as incoherent patchwork and an abomination, in his *Formula Missae* of 1523 omits everything except the *Sursum corda,* Preface, *Sanctus* and *Benedictus qui venit,* and the Words of Institution; while in his *Deutsche Messe* of 1526 consecration of the elements is not by prayer at all but by formula, the recitation of the Words of Institution being the only fragment of the ancient Canon to be retained. Calvin based his service book, *La Forme des Prières* upon Bucer's Strasbourg rite which followed the main outline of the Roman Canon, and it is from this that his Prayer of Consecration is derived. The Intercessions, however, are detached from the Canon and placed after the collection of alms. The *Anamnesis* is followed by a prayer for the reception by faith of the true body and blood of Christ and for a holy life. There is no *Sursum corda,* Preface or *Sanctus,* and the Words of Institution are read as a warrant following the Consecration Prayer. John Knox's *The Forme of Prayers* follows Calvin closely but not slavishly. His Prayer of Consecration consists of Adoration leading to Thanksgiving for creation and redemption, an *Anamnesis* and a doxology.

These Reformation rites have one common weakness—each of them perpetuates the Roman lack of an *Epiclesis* which had been central in the classical form of the Consecration Prayer. The one exception is Cranmer's Communion Office in the 1549 Book of Common Prayer. Cranmer, who was one of the ablest liturgical scholars of his day, was acquainted with Eastern, as well as Western, traditions of worship. Retaining as much as possible of the medieval

[1] ibid., p. 73.

rite, he restored order to the dislocated Roman Canon, and into it he inserted an *Epiclesis* based upon the Greek Liturgy of St. Basil. Unhappily this was removed in the 1552 Prayer Book and never restored in subsequent editions; hence the Anglican Consecration Prayer has remained incomplete ever since.[1]

It is to Scotland that we owe the restoration of wholeness in the Reformed rites. Although the *Epiclesis* does not appear in Knox's Consecration Prayer, it had always had a place in the old Celtic rites,[2] and Maxwell maintains that 'there are grounds for believing that its use never quite died out in Scotland. In any case, the lack of an *epiclesis* was soon generally felt, and though one does not appear in the texts until later, there is evidence that an *epiclesis* was comparatively early supplied in practice. . . . An *epiclesis* appears in most Scottish forms from "Laud's Liturgy" and the Westminster Directory to the present day.'[3]

The worship of the English Puritans, as we have seen, followed the pattern of Geneva, and John Knox's *The Forme of Prayers* was widely used until the Westminster Directory appeared in 1644. Hence the Consecration Prayer in the English Presbyterian rite has not differed in essentials from the Scottish use. The Independents, however, following the early Brownist practice, had a separate consecration of each of the elements.[4] First the bread was blessed and

[1] The *Anamnesis* also was removed in 1552, further impoverishing the Anglican rite. Both *Anamnesis* and *Epiclesis* are restored in the proposed revision of 1928.

[2] These belong to the Gallican family in which the *Epiclesis* was retained.

[3] op. cit., pp. 124-5.

[4] See Baillie, *A Dissuasive,* p. 121: 'They have also learned from the Brownists a double and distinct consecration, one for every element apart,'

distributed and then the wine, so following literally the actions of our Lord at the Last Supper.[1] 'This,' comments Horton Davies, 'is an example of the blind devotion of the Puritans to the very letter of the Scriptures. It is also a singular proof of their belief in the Real Presence.[2] Baxter's 'Savoy Liturgy' of 1661 makes provision for double consecration, if desired, and the practice still continues in some Congregational and Baptist churches. It is, however, a departure from both primitive and Reformed traditions, and in Congregationalism it is increasingly giving place to the classical form of the Consecration Prayer. In Methodist churches Wesley's revision of the Communion Office in the Book of Common Prayer is normally used. Hence the Consecration Prayer, which is virtually that of the 1662 Prayer Book, lacks the completeness of the classical form.

In 1925 the Canadian Congregational, Methodist and Presbyterian Churches came together to form the United Church of Canada which published its *Book of Common Order* in 1932. The aim of the compilers, as stated in the Preface, has been to set forth 'orders that are loyal to the Spirit of Christ and loyal to the experience of the Church of all ages and of all lands,' and also 'carry on the devotional usage of the three uniting Communions in their living integrity.' Their notable achievement is focused in the Order for the Celebration of the Lord's Supper or Holy Communion, which, as Maxwell points out, felicitously combines elements from the traditions of both East and West. The Consecration Prayer is based upon Cranmer's classical form in the 1549 Prayer Book but 'enriched by including in the

[1] See Cotton, *The Way of the Churches of Christ in New England*, pp. 68-69, for a description of this Independent practice.

[2] *The Worship of the English Puritans*, pp. 208-9.

ordinary preface a brief thanksgiving for creation and providence, as in Primitive and Eastern use.'[1] The *Epiclesis* is from the Church of Scotland *Prayers for Divine Service* as are also the Intercessions which may be used either after the Offertory or at the end of the Consecration Prayer. Here is the Prayer, a model for the climax of Free Church worship:

Minister: The Lord be with you.
People: And with thy spirit.
Minister: Lift up your hearts;
People: We lift them up unto the Lord.
Minister: Let us give thanks unto our Lord God;
People: It is meet and right so to do.

It is very meet, right, and our bounden duty, that we should at all times, and in all places, give thanks unto thee, O Holy Lord, Father Almighty, Everlasting God, who didst create the heavens and the earth and all that in them is, who didst make man in thine own image, and whose tender mercies are over all thy works.

(*Here may follow one of the proper Prefaces*)

Therefore with angels and archangels and with all the company of heaven, we laud and magnify thy glorious name; evermore praising thee, and saying,

Holy, holy, holy, Lord God of hosts,
Heaven and earth are full of thy glory.
Glory be to thee, O Lord most high.

All glory and thanksgiving be to thee, Almighty God, our heavenly Father, for that thou of thy tender mercy didst give thine only Son Jesus Christ to take our nature upon him, to suffer death upon the Cross for our redemption; who made there a full, perfect, and sufficient sacrifice for the sins of the whole world; and did institute, and in his holy Gospel, com-

[1] W. D. Maxwell, op. cit., p. 162.

mand us to continue, a perpetual memory of that his precious death until his coming again.

Who, the same night in which he was betrayed, took bread, and when he had given thanks, he brake it, and said, Take, eat, this is my Body, which is broken for you; this do in remembrance of me. After the same manner also he took the cup, saying, This cup is the new Covenant in my Blood; this do ye, as oft as ye drink it, in remembrance of me.

Wherefore, having in remembrance his precious death and passion, his glorious resurrection and ascension, and pleading his eternal sacrifice, we thy servants do set forth this memorial which he hath willed us to make, giving thee thanks that thou hast counted us worthy to stand before thee.

And we most humbly beseech thee, O merciful Father, to vouchsafe unto us thy gracious presence, and so to sanctify with thy Word and Spirit these thine own gifts of bread and wine which we set before thee, that the bread which we break may be to us the Communion of the Body of Christ, and the cup of blessing which we bless the Communion of the Blood of Christ.

And we entirely desire thy fatherly goodness mercifully to accept this our sacrifice of praise and thanksgiving; most humbly beseeching thee to grant, that by the merits and death of thy Son Jesus Christ, we and thy whole Church may obtain remission of our sins, and all other benefits of his passion.

And here we offer and present unto thee, O Lord, ourselves, our souls and bodies, to be a reasonable, holy, and living sacrifice unto thee: humbly beseeching thee, that all we, who are partakers of this Holy Communion, may be fulfilled with thy grace and heavenly benediction.

And although we be unworthy, through our manifold sins, to offer unto thee any sacrifice, yet we beseech thee to accept this our bounden duty and service, not weighing our merits, but pardoning our offences;

Through Jesus Christ our Lord, by whom, and with whom

in the unity of the Holy Spirit, all honour and glory be unto thee, O Father Almighty, world without end. Amen.

(*Here may follow the Intercessions, if not used earlier*)

And now, as our Saviour Christ hath taught us, we say, Our Father. . . .

With this may be compared another even more recent liturgical achievement—the Church of South India's Order for the Lord's Supper, first published in June 1950 and approved in its revised form by the Synod in January 1954 for general use where it is desired. Here is a remarkable liturgy, classical in form yet combining elements drawn from many traditions, and springing directly out of the fusion of Anglican, Congregational, Methodist and Presbyterian devotional life. The ancient Deacon's Litany is restored; the essential symbolism of the Little and Great Entrances is retained. 'At the same time, there is room for variety of ceremony and administration in accordance with long-established customs in the different parts of our Church.' Besides the provision of alternative forms, 'there is opportunity for free prayer and for silent prayer.' A notable feature is that 'a large and essential part in the Liturgy is given to the congregation, even in the Eucharistic Prayer, for every member of the Church has his own part in the action of the Eucharist.' The underlying principle of the Order is that in the expression of the Church's response of praise and prayer to the gracious act of God 'we act together as one body in Christ.' Hence 'some parts are given, not to the presbyter, but to the "deacon" or to the congregation as a whole.'[1]

As in the Order of the United Church of Canada, the Consecration Prayer is based upon Cranmer's classical form

[1] See Introduction, pp. iii-iv.

of 1549, except that Oblation follows Communion as in the 1552 Prayer Book.[1] A general preface of thanksgiving for creation and redemption is added, for which may be substituted a preface proper to the season of the Christian Year. In addition to joining in the *Sanctus* and the *Benedictus qui venit,* the congregation makes two responses. The first of these follows the recital of the Words of Institution:

Amen. Thy death, O Lord, we commemorate, thy resurrection we confess, and thy second coming we await. Glory be to thee, O Christ.

The second response comes after the *Anamnesis:*

We give thanks to thee, we praise thee, we glorify thee, O Lord our God.

The prayer concludes with the *Epiclesis* and a doxology, after which the congregation join in saying the Lord's Prayer. Then, after a brief silence, there follows the Prayer of Humble Access, said by all, the Fraction, and Communion. Communion is followed by Oblation. This is not optional, as in the Book of Common Prayer, but is included in *both* of the alternative post-communion prayers.

The Great Prayer of Thanksgiving and Consecration is not only central in the Lord's Supper. As Maxwell reminds us, it 'provides a model that may be used at other high acts of thanksgiving and consecration. Thus it is particularly appropriate at the ordination of Ministers, the consecration of a church, the solemnization of Christian marriage, the burial of the dead, a national thanksgiving, and the sanctification of water at baptism. . . . No form could be more appropriate for such occasions, and none can so perfectly express the gratitude and praise of fervent worshippers.'[2]

[1] See pp. 30-31.

[2] *Concerning Worship,* pp. 145-9.

3. *The Manual Acts* of breaking the bread and taking the cup of poured out wine reproduce the very heart of our Lord's prophetic symbolism in this third act of the Upper Room. Its significance has been finely expressed by P. T. Forsyth[1]:

The bread was broken. It *must* be broken. The loaf cannot be eaten whole. So it was a spiritual necessity, a necessity in God, that Christ should die. . . . Just as truly as food must be destroyed before it can be of use to us, so *He* had to be destroyed before *He* could savingly serve us. *We must be broken ere we deeply bless.* Self-will, self-seeking, self-love must be broken (by whatever judgments) in a divine love, else every other contribution we may offer, even for the purposes of Christ, is rejected by God. . . . As Christ broke His bread, so He gave His body to be broken. As His body was broken, so was His heart. As His heart was broken, so was His self-will. Without this breaking there is no redemption, no share in redemption. So also (and pointing the tragedy and inwardness of the rite rather than adding a second half—since the blood is part of the body) without shedding of blood there is no remission of sins. . . . There is, indeed, no intrinsic sanctity, whatever eloquence, in the bread or wine. The elements are suggestive instruments, but the real effect is in the act. The sanctity is in the act of breaking, of pouring out; the real sanctity was in the deed of broken heart and will, that outpouring of the central soul, of which such procedure was but the outward sign.

The Fraction, as this action came to be called,[2] had such prominence in the primitive rite that the latter became known as 'the breaking of bread.' It figures in every classic liturgy, Eastern and Western, Catholic and Reformed. One of the concerns of the Reformers was to restore it to its

[1] op. cit., pp. 239-40.

[2] Strictly speaking, the Fraction means only the breaking of the bread. The term is used comprehensively for the Manual Acts, however, and therefore includes the taking of the cup.

original prominence by stripping away the superfluous ceremonial of the Mass and insisting that the minister stand *behind* the Holy Table so that his actions might be clearly seen. It is prescribed in the *Westminster Confession* and the *Savoy Declaration* no less clearly than by the rubrics of the Book of Common Prayer.[1] And yet, ironically enough, during this last half century the Manual Acts have completely disappeared from many, if not most, Free Church celebrations of the Lord's Supper.

Two factors have contributed to this neglect of a vital part of the Supper. In the first place, the gains of the Oxford Movement in the Anglican Church aroused in many Free Churchmen a strong suspicion of what is popularly (although wrongly) called 'ritualism.' All the same, as E. R. Micklem comments, 'it would seem a curious excess of Puritanism which makes Christ's disciples look askance at the "ritualistic" actions of their Lord.'[2] Secondly, the Free Church innovation of individual cups and ready-cut bread has complicated the issue. The simple yet dignified ceremonial of breaking a loaf and holding up a cup becomes almost ludicrous when fifty or more quarter-inch cubes of bread are substituted for the one loaf and trays of liqueur glasses replace the common cup. All very hygienic, no doubt; but if our hygienic scruples impoverish the supreme means of grace, they profit us nothing.[3]

The Church, if it be true to its trust, must celebrate the Gospel Sacraments according to the ordinance of Christ.

[1] See *West. Con.*, ch. XXIX. iii and *Sav. Decl.*, ch. XXX. iii.

[2] *Our Approach to God*, p. 261.

[3] Unfortunately these scruples have been exploited for commercial purposes, e.g. the almost blasphemous advertisement: 'There's Death in the Communion Cup! Has your Church adopted Individual Cups?'

And 'in so far as Scripture is our norm, we may as little diminish as increase the ritual acts there indicated.'[1] We have no reason to doubt that when our Lord broke the bread and took the cup and said, 'This *do* . . .' He meant what He said. Free Church ministers will do well therefore to heed E. R. Micklem's salutary warning: 'The Lord's dramatic symbolism is not properly represented if the minister merely repeats the words of institution, and then hands out the bread and wine to the serving deacons. It is his duty to take bread and break it in the sight of the assembled communicants, and likewise to take the cup and present it as he speaks the words concerning it.'[2] If we must have individual cups and ready-cut bread, at least there may also be provided a piece of bread suitable for the minister to break, and the chalice can be put upon the Table so that it may be raised at the appropriate place.

The proper place in the service for the Manual Acts is between the Consecration Prayer and the delivery of the elements, thus preserving the correct sequence of our Lord's acts in the Upper Room: 'He took,' 'He gave thanks,' 'He brake,' 'He gave.' They occur here in the primitive rite and in the general custom of both East and West. The Anglican rites are an exception. Here the Manual Acts accompany the recitation of the Words of Institution in the Consecration Prayer. This, however, is a liturgical defect which is to be deplored.[3] The Fraction forms a distinct and vital part

[1] N. Micklem, *Christian Worship*, p. 254.

[2] op. cit., p. 261.

[3] According to Brightman, the Fraction is included in the Consecration Prayer in only two Eastern rites, the Coptic and the Abyssinian. See *Lit. E. & W.*, pp. 177, 233. Maxwell points out that in the Sarum rite it is expressly forbidden during the Consecration Prayer. *Concerning Worship*, p. 20.

of the action of the Supper. Its dramatic symbolism is obscured if it is embedded in the Consecration Prayer which should precede it or telescoped into the delivery of the elements which follows. 'It stands alone as a dramatic action of great significance.'[1] At the conclusion of the Lord's Prayer the minister should repeat the Words of Institution, taking and breaking the bread at the appropriate places, and holding up the chalice at the mention of the cup. He then proceeds to the final act of the Supper to which we now turn.

4. *The Delivery and Reception* of the consecrated bread and wine complete the symbolic action of the Upper Room. The full significance of this final act of Communion can be seen only against the background of Old Testament sacrifice.[2] It derives its meaning from the sacred meal which was the last stage in the sacrificial ritual.

Why were animal sacrifices offered by the ancient People of God? What is the significance of this ritual of blood-shedding, so strange and indeed repulsive to the modern mind? Sacrifice was for the Israelite the divinely ordained means of approach to God, the sacramental 'means of grace' by which the covenant relationship of God and His People was maintained. Through it the penitent sinner seeking reconciliation and restoration could draw near to the Holy God and receive the sign and seal of His forgiveness. There is no thought of 'propitiation' here; the decisive action is God's, not man's. Whereas in pagan sacrifice the emphasis is upon what man can do to win the favour of God, Hebrew sacrifice is based upon what God does for man. It is a signi-

[1] W. D. Maxwell, *Concerning Worship,* p. 20.

[2] I have discussed Sacrifice more fully in my book, *The Nature and Authority of the Bible* (James Clarke), chapter VI. ii. 6.

ficant fact that God is never the object of the Hebrew verb translated 'to propitiate' or 'to expiate.' In the Old Testament sacrifices it is not man who 'propitiates' God but God who 'expiates' or 'covers' man's sin in his own appointed way.

In sacrifice sinful man uses this symbolic means which God Himself has provided as the vehicle of His forgiving, restoring grace. It expresses, at one and the same time, both the divine initiative in redemption and the complementary human response. Its essence is the identification of the worshipper with his offering. Bishop Hicks has made this plain in his illuminating analysis of the six stages of the sacrificial ritual.[1] First, the penitent worshipper seeking reconciliation with God 'draws near' with his offering. Second, he lays his hands on the animal's head, thus identifying himself with the sacrificial victim: what happens henceforth to it is the outward and visible sign of what happens inwardly and spiritually to himself. Then he kills the animal: its blood, the symbol of its life, is released so that it may be surrendered to God. But since he is identified with it, its death is his death and the shedding of its blood the symbolic surrendering of his own life to God. The blood, the surrendered life, is then taken by the priest into the presence of God and so Atonement is made—God and man become at one. The body of the victim may now be offered on the altar. Its burning symbolizes the worshipper's offering of himself, utterly and completely, to God. The fire, the sign of God's acceptance, transforms rather than destroys it; that which was carnal and earthly becomes sublimated and spiritualized so that it can ascend as smoke to the heavenly dwelling-place of God. Finally, the flesh of the animal is eaten by

[1] F. C. N. Hicks, *The Fulness of Sacrifice*, pp. 13-14.

the worshipper and his family, or members of the community, at a ritual meal. 'Now that the rebel life has been surrendered and forgiven; now that the carnal man has been transformed into spirit through self-offering, not only God and man, but man and man—all who are worshipping there at that altar—become one, in the holy meal.'[1]

The New Testament writers, as their language plainly indicates, interpreted the Cross in terms of sacrifice. Not only so, but our Lord Himself equally clearly regarded His death as a sacrifice and instituted the sacrament of Holy Communion as a means whereby His disciples might participate in the power of His surrendered life.[2] Man is not self-sufficient. We live only by what we receive from the universe beyond us. Just as our bodies require bread to sustain physical life, so also our souls are dependent for spiritual nourishment upon the life of God given to men in Jesus Christ. But life, as Otto Fricke reminds us, is only possible on the basis of sacrifice. 'All nourishment is sacrificed life.'[3] We have bread because the corn of wheat dies; we have wine because the grape bleeds. 'I am the bread of life,' says Jesus. 'The bread that I will give is my flesh, which I will give for the life of the world.' 'Except ye eat the flesh of the Son of man, and drink his blood, ye have no life in you' (Jn. vi.). 'To us,' says an early Christian liturgy, 'Thou hast given spiritual food and drink through thy Servant.'[4]

[1] J. S. Whale, *Christian Doctrine,* pp. 83-84. I am deeply indebted to Dr. Whale's teaching in this section.

[2] See Vincent Taylor, *Jesus and His Sacrifice.*

[3] *Die Sakramente in der protestantischen Kirche,* p. 38, quoted by J. S. Whale, *What is a Living Church?* p. 56 n.

[4] *Didache,* x. 3.

> The Servant [comments J. S. Whale] is the Lamb of God who comes with us as we draw near to the Altar of God. He makes himself one with us in the Incarnation. We sinners kill our Victim; the Crucified takes his blood, his surrendered, outpoured life, now our life through our identification with him, through the veil of his broken flesh into God's very presence. He atones for us. In the offering of his Manhood, our separate manhoods, conjoined with his, are also offered to God in eternal service. God accepts the offering by the fire of his Spirit, and so transforms it. Thus does he receive us at his Board, the Table of the Lord which is the earthly image of the heavenly Altar. The very life of God, the Creator and the Redeemer, is here made available to us, through the Holy Spirit. We celebrate the mystery of life as corporate communion in and with the eternal God.[1]

Through partaking in faith of the emblems of our Lord's body and blood, we both identify ourselves with His self-offering and receive Christ Himself with all the benefits of His Passion. And we do so not in isolation but together. This sacrament is called the *Communion* of the Lord's Supper because in it we share with others in the divine life of the Crucified and Risen Lord. It is in fellowship, not only with Christ but also with one another, that we receive at His Table nourishment unto eternal life. 'We are one body because we partake of the same bread; and that bread is to us the life of God, by which we all live.'[2] This unity of Christians in the fellowship of the Lord's Supper is expressed symbolically by the one loaf and the single chalice. That is the meaning of St. Paul's words in 1 Cor. x. 16-17: 'The

[1] *Christian Doctrine,* p. 168.

[2] C. H. Dodd, 'The Sacrament of the Lord's Supper in the New Testament' in *Christian Worship* (Ed. N. Micklem), pp. 80-81.

cup of blessing which we bless, is it not the communion of the blood of Christ? The bread which we break, is it not the communion of the body of Christ? For we being many are one bread, and one body: for we are all partakers of that one bread.'

Here is the basis of the objection to individual cups and ready-cut bread. Not only do they stultify the Manual Acts; they symbolize the wrong things. They are indeed a denial of the very unity which the Supper is intended to express. E. R. Micklem points out that 'the solecism of individual cups is far more serious in churches which hold a Protestant view about the nature of the sacrament than it would be in churches holding a "Catholic" view, because for the Protestant the sacrament is the whole ceremony with its symbols and its actions, and the word is not to be applied to the consecrated elements alone. . . . It is difficult to conceive anything much less suggestive of the one loaf than the Catholic wafer, and Protestants object to it for that reason; but are Nonconformist "individual cups" a whit more suggestive of the one chalice? To the Catholic this may not be of great importance, but to the Protestant it is.'[1] It is all the more necessary, therefore, when individual cups and cut bread are used, for a chalice and a loaf—or at least a large piece of bread—to be placed on the Table so that something of the correct symbolism of the Supper may be preserved.

There are two alternative modes of distributing the bread and wine. In ancient ecclesiastical practice the communicants came forward to the sanctuary and received the elements at the Holy Table, the celebrant administering the bread and a deacon the cup. The early custom—still retained in the Greek Church—was for the people to receive

[1] op. cit., pp. 264-5.

standing. In England prior to the Reformation, however, it was customary to receive communion kneeling. Both practices were retained in the Reformed rites of Strasbourg and Geneva. 'Communion at Strasbourg was received standing or kneeling, the people going forward to the Holy Table. The celebrant stood at the north end of the Holy Table to give the Bread, and the assisting minister stood at the south end to minister the Cup. The communicants formed a continuous line down the central passage of the nave, coming slowly forward to receive first the Bread then the Wine, and so returning to their places.'[1] Similarly, in Calvin's Geneva rite 'communion was received standing or kneeling, the people coming forward to the Holy Table, where, as at Strasbourg, they received the Bread from one minister and the Cup from another.'[2] This is the practice of the Anglican and Methodist Churches. Frequently, however, only one minister will communicate the people; and it is the custom to receive kneeling. The communicants leave their places and kneel at the sanctuary rail, receiving the bread in the cupped right hand which is supported in the left.

In the other mode of distribution the communicants remain in their places, the bread and wine being brought to them from the sanctuary by the elders or deacons. This practice, which was introduced by Zwingli at Zurich, became general among English Nonconformists in the seventeenth century and was later adopted in Scotland. It is now the established custom in the Baptist, Congregational, and Presbyterian Churches and can claim ancient precedent in Justin Martyr's classic description of second century worship

[1] W. D. Maxwell, *An Outline of Christian Worship*, p. 111.

[2] ibid., p. 119.

at Rome.[1] Communion is received sitting, as if around the Lord's Table. This symbolism is emphasized by the Presbyterian practice of covering the book-boards of the pews with white linen 'houselling cloths': each represents an extension of the Holy Table.[2]

J. R. P. Sclater points out that the first of these methods of distribution emphasizes the individual meaning of the sacrament, since each communicant must go forward to the Holy Table and receive the elements separately. In the second, however, its communal aspect is to the fore: the whole membership of the Church, served by its elders, is seated about the Table of the Lord. He suggests, therefore, a synthesis of both practices; the first being more suitable for frequent communion while reserving the second for great churchly celebrations of the Lord's Supper once or twice a year.[3]

The correct order in the distribution of the elements is for the celebrant to receive first, communicating himself in both kinds. This, as Maxwell points out, has been the universal practice from earliest times. It was retained by all the Reformers and is explicitly laid down in Calvin's *Form of Prayers* (and the modern Genevan *Liturgie*), the West-

[1] 'After the President has given thanks and all the people have said Amen, those among us who are called deacons give to all present, sharing it among them, the bread and wine mixed with water over which thanks have been given.' See *First Apology,* lxv-lxvii.

[2] 'Houselling cloths,' together with 'houselling benches,' were in use in England before the Reformation and are associated with the medieval practice of communicating only once a year. The communicant lifted the cloth as he received so that no particle of the consecrated element might fall to the ground. As now used in Presbyterian Churches, however, they are a relic of the ancient Scottish Reformed practice of placing in the quire or nave a long Communion Table at which the communicants, when they came forward, sat.

[3] *The Public Worship of God.,* pp. 164ff.

minster *Directory*, Baxter's 'Savoy Liturgy,' and the Scottish *Book of Common Order* (1940). The modern practice of the minister's being served after the people by a senior elder or deacon is the result of confusing liturgical principles with dining room etiquette. 'The Minister is not the host at the holy Table, as he would be at his own dinner table, and he is not to behave as if he were the host. Our Lord is the host, and all, including the Minister, receive from Him. It is the Minister's office to set an example to the people; and he should communicate himself, as receiving from the Lord's hands—he alone at the holy Table is an ordained Minister.'[1] The function of elders or deacons at the Holy Table is not to serve the minister but to assist him in the distribution of the bread and wine. The minister, therefore, after communicating himself, gives them communion in both kinds before handing to them the consecrated elements for delivery to the people.

The bread and wine, Maxwell maintains, should be distributed together, the elders or deacons who deliver the wine following as closely as possible those who are distributing the bread. 'There should not be two separate actions in the communion of the people in both kinds, and there should be no delay between the deliveries.'[2] The people should communicate in each kind as soon as they receive it, not waiting until all have been served and then eating or drinking together as is frequently done when individual cups are used. This common practice of 'simultaneous communion,' doubtless intended to emphasize the corporate nature of the act, introduces a distracting artificial element into the ser-

[1] W. D. Maxwell, *Concerning Worship*, p. 60.

[2] ibid., p. 61.

vice. Consuming the wine together from individual cups is too reminiscent of drinking a toast.[1]

The appropriate words of delivery are said by the minister as he gives each of the elements to the people, whether directly at the sanctuary rail or through the serving elders or deacons who distribute them in the pews. The general custom in Free Church celebrations is to use only a scriptural form:

Take, eat; this is the body of Christ which is broken for you; do this in remembrance of Him.

This cup is the new covenant in the blood of Christ, which is shed for the remission of the sins of many; drink ye all of it.

There is much to be said, however, for the classic Anglican form, expressing as it does through its historic conflation:[2] both the objective and subjective aspects of the sacrament:

The body of our Lord Jesus Christ, which was given for thee, preserve thy body and soul unto everlasting life. Take and eat this in remembrance that Christ died for thee, and feed on Him in thy heart by faith with thanksgiving.

The blood of our Lord Jesus Christ, which was shed for thee, preserve thy body and soul unto everlasting life. Drink this in remembrance that Christ's blood was shed for thee, and be thankful.

This fourth and final act of the Lord's Supper has been traditionally accompanied by the singing of psalms or the *Agnus Dei*. Here was the place of the ancient communion chant in the Mass, and the practice of singing psalms during the communion of the people was favoured by the Reformers. Psalms or hymns were sung in Luther's *Deutsche Messe* and Calvin's Strasbourg rite. At Geneva, however, Calvin replaced the communion psalm by the reading of passages

[1] Maxwell describes 'simultaneous communion' as 'a burlesque that destroys devotion'—ibid., p. 61, note 1.

[2] See p. 32.

of Scripture, a practice in which he was followed by John Knox who stipulated that the minister should read 'the whole historie of the Passion' at the people's communion. In most Free Churches both of these practices have now given place to a period of silence during the delivery and reception of the elements. Sometimes very soft organ music is played, especially when there is a large number of communicants. At such times the *Agnus Dei* or some other suitable hymn might well be quietly sung by the choir unaccompanied, as Maxwell suggests. But many Free Churchmen regard complete silence as the most appropriate setting for this solemn act.

The service should end, however, on a note of praise. This, indeed, should be its dominant note throughout. It is not a sad recollection of a dead Jesus but an act of joyful and adoring fellowship with a Risen, Glorified Lord. The Eucharist is no mere re-enactment of the Last Supper: the Upper Room and the Cross are transfigured in the light of Easter Morning. We show forth the death of One who has broken the bonds of death, the Lord of Life whom death could not hold. It is a significant fact that the early Church celebrated the Lord's Supper 'not on Thursday night, the time of its institution, or on Friday afternoon, the time when our Lord died upon the Cross, but on Sunday morning, the time of His resurrection.' 'The glory of the Lord shines round about it, as in this supreme act of Christian worship men offer to Him an oblation of all possible praise, showing forth His death and victory, rejoicing in His real presence among them, and looking for His coming again to judge the world in righteousness.'[1]

[1] Quotations from W. D. Maxwell, *Concerning Worship,* pp. 13, 15-16, to whom I am closely indebted in this paragraph.

BOOKS FOR FURTHER READING

Guidance for further reading may be found in the following selected list, which is intended for the general reader rather than for the specialist. Larger or more advanced works are marked with an asterisk. Publishers given are the British publishers (if any): in other countries the books may be issued by different firms. It cannot be assumed that all books listed are in print.

A more comprehensive bibliography is given in *An Outline of Christian Worship* by W. D. Maxwell.

I THE THEORY AND PRACTICE OF WORSHIP

COFFIN, H. S., *The Public Worship of God* (Independent Press).
DEARMER, P., *The Art of Public Worship* (Mowbrays).
*DIX, G., *The Shape of the Liturgy* (Dacre Press: A. & C. Black).
DOBSON, J. O., *Worship* (S.C.M. Press).
HEBERT, A. G., *Liturgy and Society* (Faber).
KAY, J. A., *The Nature of Christian Worship* (Epworth Press).
MAXWELL, W. D., *Concerning Worship* (Oxford U.P.).
MICKLEM, E. R., *Our Approach to God* (Hodder & Stoughton).
MICKLEM, N. (Editor), *Christian Worship* (Oxford U.P.).
RATTENBURY, J. E., *Vital Elements of Public Worship* (Epworth Press).
SCLATER, J. R. P., *The Public Worship of God* (Hodder & Stoughton).
SCOTT, C. A., *The Church, its Worship and Sacraments* (S.C.M. Press).
*THEOLOGICAL COMMISSION OF FAITH AND ORDER, *Ways of Worship* (S.C.M. Press).
*UNDERHILL, E., *Worship* (Nisbet).

II THE HISTORY OF WORSHIP

BURKITT, F. C., *Christian Worship* (Cambridge U.P.).
*CLARKE and HARRIS (Editors), *Liturgy and Worship* (S.P.C.K.).
CULLMANN, O., *Early Christian Worship* (S.C.M. Press).
DAVIES, H., *The Worship of the English Puritans* (Dacre Press: A. & C. Black).
*DUCHESNE, L., *Christian Worship, its Origin and Evolution* (S.P.C.K).
HARRISON, D. E. W., *The Book of Common Prayer* (Canterbury Press).
HEILER, F., *The Spirit of Worship* (Hodder & Stoughton).

HISLOP, D. H., *Our Heritage of Public Worship* (T. & T. Clark).
MACDONALD, A. B., *Christian Worship in the Primitive Church* (T. & T. Clark).
MAXWELL, W. D., *John Knox's Genevan Service Book* (Oliver & Boyd).
— , *An Outline of Christian Worship* (Oxford U.P.).
MICKLEM, N. (Editor), *Christian Worship*, Part II (Oxford U.P.).
PHILLIPS, C. S., *The Background of the Prayer Book* (S.P.C.K.).
*PROCTER and FRERE, *A New History of the Book of Common Prayer* (Macmillan).
*SRAWLEY, J. H., *The Early History of the Liturgy* (Cambridge U.P.).

III PREACHING

BROOKS, P., *Lectures on Preaching* (Allenson).
COGGAN, F. D., *The Ministry of the Word* (Canterbury Press).
DALE, R. W., *Nine Lectures on Preaching* (Hodder & Stoughton).
FARMER, H. H., *The Servant of the Word* (Nisbet).
FORSYTH, P. T., *Positive Preaching and the Modern Mind* (Independent Press).
JOWETT, J. H., *The Preacher, his Life and Work* (Hodder & Stoughton).
STEWART, J. S., *Heralds of God* (Hodder & Stoughton).

IV PUBLIC PRAYER

MAXWELL, W. D., *Concerning Worship*, Appendix A (Oxford U.P.). and the relevant chapters of books in Section 1.

The following contemporary service books provide valuable assistance in the preparation of Public Prayer:

A Book of Public Worship, Huxtable, Marsh, Micklem & Todd (Oxford U.P.).
Devotional Services, John Hunter (Dent).
Prayers and Services for Christian Festivals, J. M. Todd (Oxford U.P.).
Prayers for Divine Service, of the Church of Scotland (Oxford U.P.).
Prayers for Parish Worship, C. F. Miller (Oxford U.P.).
Prayers for the Christian Year, of the Church of Scotland (Oxford U.P.).
The Book of Common Order of the Church of Scotland (Oxford U.P.).
The Book of Common Order, of the United Church of Canada (Toronto).
The Book of Common Prayer as Proposed in 1928 (Oxford U.P.).

The Book of Common Worship, of the Presbyterian Church in the U.S.A. (Philadelphia).

The Directory for Public Worship, of the Presbyterian Church of England (London).

The Presbyterian Service Book, of the Presbyterian Churches of England and Wales (London).

V CHURCH MUSIC AND ARCHITECTURE

*BENSON, L. F., *The English Hymn* (Hodder and Stoughton).

DAVIES and GRACE, *Music and Worship* (Eyre & Spottiswoode).

*DOUGLAS, W., *Church Music in History and Practice* (Scribners).

*DRUMMOND, A. L., *The Church Architecture of Protestantism* (T. & T. Clark).

MANNING, B. L., *The Hymns of Wesley and Watts* (Independent Press).

MAXWELL, W. D., *Concerning Worship,* chap. 19, 'The Church Building' (Oxford U.P.).

ROUTLEY, E., *The Church and Music* (Duckworth).

— , *Hymns and Human Life* (John Murray).

VI THE SACRAMENTS

BARCLAY, A., *The Protestant Doctrine of the Lord's Supper* (Jackson, Son, & Co., Glasgow).

*DIX, G., *The Shape of the Liturgy* (Dacre Press: A. & C. Black).

FORSYTH, P. T., *The Church and the Sacraments* (Independent Press).

*HEADLAM and DUNKERLEY (Editors), *The Ministry and the Sacraments* (S.C.M. Press).

MAXWELL, W. D., *Concerning Worship,* ch. 4-6 (Oxford U.P.).

MICKLEM, N. (Editor), *Christian Worship,* ch. V and XV (Oxford U.P.).

SCOTT, C. A., *The Church, its Worship and Sacraments* (S.C.M. Press), ch. III.

WHALE, J. S., *Christian Doctrine,* ch. VII (Cambridge U.P.).

INDEX

Absolution, 90, 102
Addai, Canons of, 50 n.
Adoration, 87-88, 100, 102, 106, 134, 168
Agapē, 16
Alms, 161
Ambrose, St., 117, 127, 131
Anabaptists, 37
Anamnēsis, 165, 166, 168, 174
Anglicans, 8, 28-35
Anselm, St., 1
Ante-Communion, 28, 39, 40, 105
Anthem, 3, 26, 107, 128
Apostolic Constitutions, 9 n., 21 n.
Augustine, St., 117, 119-20, 139, 165

Baillie, Robert, 169 n.
Bancroft, Richard, 108 n.
Baptism, 3, 138-9, 140, 141, 142-53
Baptists, 38, 40, 108, 137, 162, 163, 170, 183
Barrowists, 37
Basilican posture, 25 n., 105, 176
Baxter, Richard, 170, 185
Bayne, Peter, 109 n.
Benedictine Rule, 21, 28
Benedictus qui venit, 165 n., 166, 168, 174
Bible, a 'mode' of the Word, 46-47, 139; language of, 59-61; reading of, 21, 30, 47-53, 55-56, 98, 100, 103, 124 (*see also* Lessons); versions of, 57-59
Bidding of the Bedes, *see* Prone
Bidding Prayer, 92-93
Blessing, 99, 104, 107, 153
Book of Common Order (Church of Scotland), 57, 95, 106, 185
Book of Common Order (United Church of Canada), 56 n., 94, 170-3
Book of Common Prayer, formation, contents and character of, 28-35, 89, 95 n., 114, 130, 161, 168, 174, 176; Puritan objection to, 37, 108-9; Wesley's recension of, 115 n., 170
Book of Common Worship, 106
Book of Public Worship, 44, 57, 88, 91, 95, 103
Brabant, F. H., 13, 110, 117-18
Bread, breaking of, 15-17, 158 (*see also* Fraction); communicating in, 23, 178-87; offering of, 4, 101, 159-63
Breviary, 23, 26, 33
Brightman, F. E., 177 n.
Broadmead Records, 38
Brooks, Phillips, 82
Brownists, 37, 169
Brunner, Emil, 46
Bucer, Martin, 27, 168
Burkitt, F. C., 30, 128, 131

Cadman, W. H., 45
Cairns, David, 162
Call to Worship, 97, 100
Calvin, J., 25, 26-28, 36, 38, 107, 120, 128, 138-40, 142 n., 154-5, 168, 183, 184, 186
Canon, the, 29, 31, 130, 166, 167, 168
Carter, H. C., 82
Christian Year, the, 56-57, 78, 174
Church of South India, *Order for the Lord's Supper*, 173-4
Clement of Rome, 165 n.
Coffin, H. S., 62
Coggan, F. D., 66-67
Commemoration of the Faithful Departed, 93-94, 107
Communion, the Holy, 3, 95, 99, 140, 153-87. *See also* Eucharist *and* Lord's Supper
Communion of the Sick, 152 n.
Communion Table, 105, 107
Compline, 21, 22, 30, 106, 107

Confession, 89-90, 98, 100, 102, 106, 134
Confirmation, 152 and n.
Congregationalists, attitude to creeds, 55; in United Churches, 170, 173; orthodoxy of, 137; worship of, 39-40, 41, 44, 103, 104, 108, 162, 163, 170, 183. *See also* Independents
Consecration Prayer, 4, 9 n., 29, 90, 94, 95, 104, 163-74, 177. *See also* Canon
Cotton, John, 170 n.
Cranmer, T., 23-24, 28-34, 167, 168-9, 170, 173
Creed, Apostles', 54-55, 136-7, in the Prone, 23 n.; in worship, 53-55, 57, 137, 139; Nicene, 54-55; Puritans' objection to, 55
Cullmann, Oscar, 45

Dale, R. W., 150
Davies, D. R., 89 n.
Davies, Horton, 36 n., 37-38, 55 n., 112, 113-14, 129, 170
Davies, W. and Grace, H., 118, 121
Dearmer, Percy, 110
Deutsche Messe, 25 n., 26, 168
Didachē, 163 n., 180
Directory for Public Worship, 163
Dix, Gregory, 156
Dodd, C. H., 67, 153, 181
Double Consecration, 169-70
Douglas, W., 123
Doumergue, E., 27
Duchesne, L., 51
Drummond, A. L., 120

Eastern rites, 17-19, 25, 160, 165, 171, 175, 177, 182
Epiclēsis, 29, 31, 94, 165, 166 n., 167, 168-9, 171, 174
Eucharist, adoration of Risen Lord in, 187; conduct of, 105; derivation of name, 90; in Cranmer's reform, 29; in Methodist worship, 39-40; in Puritan worship, 38-39; norm of worship, 15-19, 97, 106; participation of congregation in, 24; Quire Offices and, 33-34; structure retained by Calvin, 27-28. *See also* Comunion *and* Lord's Supper
Euchologion, 42
Evening Prayer, *see* Evensong
Evensong, 30, 31, 33-34, 35, 106, 124

Farmer, H. H., 65-66, 76, 79, 83
Formula Missae, 26
Forsyth, P. T., 45, 46, 61-63, 64, 67, 68-69, 70, 71, 73, 84, 140-1, 158, 159, 175
Fraction, the, 174, 175-8
Franks, R. S., 17-18, 19
Frere, W. H., 128
Fricke, Otto, 180
Fuller, R. H., 61

Gallican rites, 169 n.
Gardiner, Stephen, 23-24
Gavin, F., 9 n.
General Confession, 89-90
General Thanksgiving, 90-91
Genevan Service Book, 37, 38, 109
Gloria Patri, 124
Gogol, N. B., 11
Gore, C., 159-60
Gradual, 51, 122, 123
Great Entrance, 18, 160, 162, 173

Harris, T. L., 97 n.
Harrison, D. E. W., 6, 13, 33, 49-50, 56-57, 152 n., 160, 161-2, 166-7
Hebert, A. G., 56, 161 n.
Heiler, F., 26, 43, 164, 167 n.
Henry, Matthew, 115
Hicks, F. C. N., 3 n., 179
Hippolytus, 9 n.; *Apostolic Tradition* of, 20 n.
Holy Spirit, in worship, 7-9, 13; invocation of, 29, 94. *See also Epiclēsis*
Hooker, R., 37, 99 n., 112
Houselling cloths, 184 and n.

Hymns, communion, 104; corporate praise in, 122, 127-8; in the Early Church, 126-7; Medieval and Reformation, 25-26, 128; office, 132 n.; opening, 102, 106; Puritan and Evangelical, 128-31; uses of, 131-7

Ikonostasis, 18, 160
Ikons, 11
Illumination, Prayer for, 94-95, 135
Independents, 36-39, 55, 162, 169-70. *See also* Congregationalists
Intercession, hymns of, 134-5; nature and forms of, 91-93; position of, 99, 100-1, 102-4, 107, 155; in early Eucharistic Prayers, 165; in the Roman Canon, 166; in Calvin's rite, 168; in Cranmer's 1552 Communion Office, 31; in the United Church of Canada's Communion Order, 171, 173
Invocation, hymns of, 134; prayers of, 88-89, 100, 102, 106; of the Holy Spirit, 29, 94. *See also Epiclēsis.*

Jenkins, D. T., 74, 85
Justin Martyr, 16-17, 163 n., 183-4

Kay, J. A., 7, 157-8
Kingsley, C., 117
Knox, John, 28, 37, 168, 169, 187

Lauds, 21, 22, 30
Lectionary, 33, 56, 57 and n.
Lections, *see* Lessons
Lessons, introduction and conclusion of, 52-53; place and content of, 48-52, 100, 107; reading of, 105; singing of psalms and, 50-52, 123-4, 126; Word proclaimed in, 3, 103, 139, 155. *See also* Bible, reading of
Litany, 34, 108; Deacon's, 173
Little Entrance, 18, 173
Lord's Prayer, as climax of prayers, 31, 104, 107, 165, 173, 174; as a preparation, 31 n.; in Cranmer's 1552 rite, 31, 95 n.; in the Prone, 23 n.; in Puritan worship, 37, 108; position changed in *Euchologion,* 42
Lord's Supper, a sign and seal of the Word, 138-42, 154-5; climax of worship, 101, 154-155; conduct of, 105; defective celebrations of, 156-9; Dominical authority of, 142; in Early Church, 15-17; Protestant restoration of, 24-25, 26-27, 29, 31; norm of Puritan worship, 38-39; in Methodism, 39-40; structure and contents of, 156-87; supreme means of grace, 153-4. *See also* Communion, the Holy, *and* Eucharist
Luther, M., 1, 25, 26, 36, 64, 69, 120, 128, 140, 168, 186

Maclaren, Ian, 84 n.
Manning, B. L., 128-30, 132 n., 149
Manson, T. W., 70-71
Manual Acts, 104, 175-8, 182
Marsh, John, 6-7, 39, 98, 99, 103
Mass, chants of, 51, 122, 123, 186; laity and, 23-24, 43; oblations of, 95-96, 160-1, 166, 167; preaching and Catholic view of, 64, 94-95; Quire Offices and, 19-21; Reformers and, 24-29, 175-6; Roman, 12, 43, 45, 49, 64, 120. *See also* Canon
Mattins, in Benedictine Rule, 21-22; in Cranmer's reform, 30, 31, 33-34; in Anglican practice, 35, 40; influence on Reformed worship, 41-42, 104-5; Exhortation in, 13-14; laity and, 23; psalms in, 124

Maxwell, W. D., 15, 16, 17, 23, 26, 32, 39, 41-42, 44, 50, 53 n., 106, 162 n., 166, 167, 169, 170-1, 174, 177 n., 178, 183, 185, 187
Methodists, in United Churches, 170, 173; liturgical tradition of, 39-40, 115 n., 162, 163, 170, 183; minister's position at Holy Table, 105; orthodoxy of, 137
Meyer, F. B., 74
Micklem, E. R., 12, 156, 159, 176, 177, 182
Micklem, Nathaniel, 140, 141, 143, 144, 145, 150, 154, 177
Middleburg Liturgy, 109
Miller, C. F., 43, 57 n., 99 n.
Miller, J. H., 113
Milton, John, 120-1, 131
Missal, 23
Moffatt, James, 58-59
Morgan, G. Campbell, 62, 73-74
Morning Prayer, *see* Mattins

Neill, Stephen, 72, 75
Newman, J. H., 72 and n., 135
Nocturns, 21
None, 21-22, 30

Oblation, climax of worship, 4, 101; hymns of, 135; in Cranmer's 1552 rite, 31; in the Mass, 166: Great, 95, 161, Lesser, 96, 160; in the South India rite, 174; only later confined to elements, 160; place of, 102-3, 104, 155, 165; prayers of, 95-96, 107, 172
Offering, for the sick and poor, 104; of gifts, 4, 101, 105, 107, 159-60, 163; of self, 4, 101. *See also* Oblation
Offertory, 101, 104, 105, 107, 159-63
Oman, John, 116
Owen, John, 55, 110 n., 111 n., 112
Oxford Movement, 41, 43, 176. *See also* Tractarians

Parry, K. L., 110, 120, 132 n., 132-3, 134 n.
Phillips, C. S., 22, 30, 35, 41, 132 n., 160
Phillips, J. B., 58-59
Post-Communion Prayer, 31, 104, 174
Prayer, different types of, 87-96; forms of, 107-9; free, 8 and n., 37-38, 111-16; liturgical, 7-9, 37-38, 109-11; ordering of, 96-107; position of minister leading, 105, 107 (*see also* Basilican posture); private and corporate, 85-87
Prayer Book, *see* Book of Common Prayer
Prayers and Services for Christian Festivals, 57
Prayers for the Christian Year, 57
Prayers for Divine Service, 171
Preaching, a 'mode' of the Word, 61-67, 139; biblical, 67-70; Christo-centric, 69-71; Godward reference of, 84; medieval decline in, 23; preparation for, 71-84; varieties of, 67-69. *See also* Sermon
Preface, general, 165, 168, 171, 174; proper, 171, 174
Presbyterians, Independents and, 36; in United Churches, 170, 173; orthodoxy of, 137; worship of, 37-39, 40, 41-42, 43-44, 108, 162, 163, 169, 183-184
Presbyterian Service Book, 163 n.
Priesthood, of all believers, 10-11; of Christ, 181. *See also* Sacrifice
Prime, 21-22, 30
Prone, the, 23 n., 25
Proper, 57
Prothesis, 17, 18, 160
Psalms, Christian use of, 122-6, 129; metrical, 25, 107, 123, 124, 128, 131; prose, 123, 124-5; recitation of, 21, 22, 30, 122; responsive reading

of, 51-52, 107, 125-6; singing of, 50-52, 100, 107, 119, 186
Psalter, *see* Psalms
Puritans, Hooker's criticism of, 112; not lacking in taste, 120; their objection to liturgy, 7-8, 37, 110-11; worship of, 35-39, 162, 169-70
Quire Offices, 19-22, 30, 33-34, 106, 124

Ratcliffe, E. C., 20, 124
Rattenbury, J. E., 39-40, 44, 66, 86 n., 107, 113 n., 115 n.
Real Presence, the, 154, 170, 187
Revelation, worship dependent upon, 5-7, 45, 103, 139; through history, 45-46
Richardson, Alan, 59-60, 61
Ritualism, 41, 158, 176
Roberts, Richard, 71

Sacrifice, Eucharist and, 154, 180-2; Hebrew, 2-3, 178-80; of Christ, 3, 180-1; of praise, 3, 11, 154; the Church's, 10-11.
Salutation, 164
Sanctus, the, 12, 164-5, 168, 171, 174
Savoy Declaration, 55, 150, 176
Savoy Liturgy, 109, 170, 185
Sclater, J. R. P., 100 n., 101, 184
Secret Collect, 160-1
Separatists, 36 n., 37
Sermon, classification, 67-69; contemporizes the Gospel, 60, 98, 99, 100-1; differentia of, 62-63, 65, 67; effectiveness of, 65; must be Christo-centric, 69-71; in the Divine Office, 35, 107, 163; in the Eucharist, 35, 103-6, 155, 163; Word proclaimed in, 3f., 139
Sext, 21, 22, 30
Simpson, P. Carnegie, 154
Smyth, Charles, 23 n., 24
Society of Friends, 108
Srawley, J. H., 159 n., 162 n.
Sternhold and Hopkins, 128
Stewart, J. S., 70, 75, 78, 82, 83
Strype, 36 n.
Supplication, 91-92, 100, 102, 106, 134
Sursum corda, 101, 164, 165, 168, 171
Synagogue, 15, 16

Taylor, Jeremy, 113
Taylor, Vincent, 3 n., 180 n.
Te Deum, 127
Temple, William, 82
Terce, 21, 22, 30
Thanksgiving, hymns of, 134; in Eucharistic Prayer, 101, 104, 163-74; place of, 99, 102f., 107, 155; post-communion, 104; prayers of, 90-91, 163-74
Thirty-nine Articles, 142
Todd, J. M., 57
'Torch Bible Commentaries' 80n.
Tractarians, 41, 131. *See also* Oxford Movement
Transubstantiation, 19, 64, 166

Underhill, Evelyn, 33-34

Van der Meer, F. G., 43
Versicles, 31 n., 92-93, 106
Vespers, 21-22, 30
Vigils, 21

Waldegrave Liturgy, 108 n., 109
Ward, W., 72 n.
Watts, Isaac, 111, 115, 128-9, 131, 136-7
Wellhausen, J., 2
Wesley, Charles, 39-40, 129-31, 135, 136
Wesley, John, 39-40, 44, 115 n., 129-31, 162, 170
Western rites, 17-19, 25, 160-1, 165-7, 175, 177, 183
Westminster Confession, 176
Westminster Directory, 37-38, 39, 109, 169, 184-5
Whale, J. S., 1, 24, 25, 63-64, 120, 123 n., 141-2, 145-6, 180, 181

Whyte, Alexander, 69
Williams, D. D., 9 n.
Wine, communicating in, 178-87; offering of, 4, 101, 159-163
Words of Institution, as warrant, 104, 156, 168; consecration by, 168; in Roman Canon, 166; in Reformation rites, 168; in the South India rite, 174; Manual Acts and, 177-8

Zwingli, Ulrich, 24, 183

PRINTED IN GREAT BRITAIN BY THE FOUNDRY PRESS LTD.